CAN I GET AN AMEN?

CELEBRATING THE LORD
IN EVERYDAY LIFE

CAN I GET AN AMEN?

ZANDRA VRANES & TAMU SMITH

Previously titled *Diary of Two Mad Black Mormons*

DESERET BOOK

SALT LAKE CITY, UTAH

Previously published in hardbound under the title *Diary of Two Mad Black Mormons*.

© 2019 Sistas in Zion LLC

All rights reserved. No part of this book may be reproduced in any form or by any means without permission in writing from the publisher, Deseret Book Company, at permissions@deseretbook.com or PO Box 30178, Salt Lake City, Utah 84130. This work is not an official publication of The Church of Jesus Christ of Latter-day Saints. The views expressed herein are the responsibility of the authors and do not necessarily represent the position of the Church or of Deseret Book Company.

DESERET BOOK is a registered trademark of Deseret Book Company.

Visit us at deseretbook.com

Library of Congress Cataloging-in-Publication Data

(CIP data on file)
ISBN 978-1-62972-977-0

Printed in the United States of America
PubLitho, Draper, UT

10 9 8 7 6 5 4 3 2

To Granny Lorna
My shining example of steadfast faith in the Lord
So much beauty, so few mirrors
Hope I've got your genes—
Because you're proof that black don't crack!

Love,
Zandra

In memory of
Arthur Lee and Susie-Mae Thomas
(Daddy & Mama)
Hope you get a glimpse of
how ya' girl is living

From prayer to praise
thank you for teaching me to gravitate
toward LOVE

XOXO,
Tamu

CONTENTS

WHO DAT? xi

MIC CHECK—IS THIS THING ON? xv

1. BREAKING AND ENTERING 1
   Finding Jesus in Jail 3
   Background Check 4
   Liar, Liar 6
   Check Yo'self Before You Wreck Yo'self 13
   Bounced Check 16
   Slippery Slope 18
   Hide 'n Seek 28

2. STAND 33
   Set Your Standards High So You Can Fly 35
   Susie Set the Standard 36
   Last Man Standing 42

CONTENTS

    God's Got Your Back 46

    Standing in the Streetlight 47

3. FEAST OF FAITH 51

    Got a Little, Get a Lot 53

    The First Fish Fry 54

    Ain't Nobody Drinkin' That Kool-Aid 58

    A Latter-day Saint Madea 64

    Can't Nobody Love Me like Jesus 67

4. THE NERVE TO SERVE 81

    Go Fish 83

    Hope for the Homeless 87

    People Aren't Projects 102

    Service Makes Me Nervous 104

    Why You Asking All Them Questions? 109

    Pay It Forward 111

    Do Not Pass Him By 113

5. BEGGING FOR CHANGE 117

    Spare Change 119

    Pennies from Heaven 122

    Swearing to Change 123

    Love Letting Go 132

    Fighting Forgiveness 135

CONTENTS

6. **FRIENDS AND FAMILY DISCOUNT** 143
   Dysfunctional Families Are Forever 145
   Mama Georgia Scrooged Me 151
   Misery Loves Company 163
   Hot Mess-ipe 177
   Despicable Me 179
   Bringin' the Pepper to Salt Lake 181

7. **RELATIONSHIP RECIPE** 189
   Relationship Reality Check 191
   Don't Save the Drama for Mama 193
   I've Been Deceived 201
   Relationship Status 207

DROPPIN' THE MIC 211

SHOUT OUTS 215

WHO DAT?

Right now you're probably wondering, "Who dat?" Who are the "Sistas in Zion"? You might even be making some assumptions too, thinking, "Well, they're black *and* they're Latter-day Saints. What's their experience got to do with me?" Since you've got your nose in our book, just this once we won't mind if it's also in our business.

We're Tamu and Zandra, but in the hardcover edition of this book (which was titled *Diary of Two Mad Black Mormons*), we went by Sista Beehive and Sista Laurel. Where we come from, they call fake names *aliases,* but apparently publishers like to use *pseudonyms*. In this paperback edition, we're going by our real first names. Oh, and speaking of aliases and pseudonyms, we've changed names and most everything else about events that have any drama in them, so there's no use wasting your time trying to figure out who you think we're talking about. We have also, everywhere that made sense, changed the word *Mormon* to language that follows the counsel we've been given by President Russell M. Nelson to refer to the Church and its members by names that reflect our belief in Jesus Christ.

Okay, now we'll tell you about us.

In the beginning: Genesis.

No, really, Genesis is where we met; it's a support group for black Latter-day Saints. Yeah, we know this is starting to sound crazy, but it's not what you think. The Genesis Group is an official auxiliary organization of The Church of Jesus Christ of Latter-day Saints for African American members of the Church, their families, and their friends. (Today we just call the folks at Genesis *family*.) So after we both moved to Utah and wondered where all the black people were, we found some of them and each other at Genesis.

Sisterhood is a beautiful thing because it's made up of sisters who are born as family and sisters who become family. We're pretty sure that God made us "sistas" because no parents could have handled us as sisters. So that's how sistahood began for the two of us. When Zandra moved away from Utah, Tamu suggested that we start a blog so we could keep in touch. A little apprehensive about putting all our business on the Internet, Zandra agreed, but only if we picked a nonpersonal topic. In hindsight, we realize we chose one of the most personal subjects out there—faith. But since faith was what had brought us together, it seemed to be the perfect fit. In 2009, we started Sistas in Zion, and we've been chattin' about church ever since.

Our hope for Sistas in Zion was to create a place where our friends and family of all faiths could openly converse, and we also wanted to share humorous aspects of our church culture. We know you might find it hard to believe that Latter-day Saints are funny. We are.

Fast forward to today. Sometimes we have to pinch ourselves as we reflect on how God is good—all the time. Oh, how He has blessed two sistas to become so much more than a dream and a blog.

So to answer the question "Who dat?" we're just two sistas with testimonies of the gospel of Jesus Christ. We love to laugh, and we think members of our church are hilarious, if we do say so ourselves. We don't always agree with one another, but we always love one another. We are

WHO DAT?

truly blessed to have one another as sisters, friends, and Sistas in Zion.

Can I Get an Amen?*

Tamu and Zandra

> ✱ A nod to the call and response used in some churches.

MIC CHECK—IS THIS THING ON?

Look, y'all, Disney is telling lies!

For most of us, life is not a fairytale. In our neck of the woods (and no, we are not talking about an enchanted forest), lives are not filled with talking mice, Prince Charmings, and fairy godmothers. Instead we get trials, tribulations, and miscommunications. And that "happily ever after" storybook ending sometimes feels more like "happy every so often." The truth is that life is challenging, it's full of ups and downs, and it can make you sad and drive you mad.

Have you ever read back through your diaries from when you were going through a hard time in your life? You might think, "Man, life hasn't changed much since then." Then at other times you think, "Wow! I've come so far."

MIC CHECK—IS THIS THING ON?

You're now able to see why you went through what you went through, and maybe you are even able to see what you learned from going through a particular trial.

That's kind of how life has been for us. In the thick of things, when you are really going through it, it's easy to be upset or let life drive you mad. But like Will Smith says (with his fine self): "Throughout life people will make you mad, disrespect you, and treat you bad. Let God deal with the things they do, 'cause hate in your heart will consume you too" (*Just the Two of Us* [2001], 26).

We have learned that God is trying to teach us, and He's doing it in ways that we will understand. The thing is, once you start looking for God, it's pretty much impossible not to find Him.

You see, the Lord is constantly reaching out towards us, and as we reach back through searching and pondering and praying, we see the Lord's lessons for us. We see them everywhere and everyday.

It's a beautiful thing to know that the Lord is always with us, that He cares enough to teach us constantly, that He's always refining us, like you would gold, because we are precious to Him. It's hard to stay mad once you realize that you're too blessed to be stressed. Today, when we turn back through the pages of the diaries of our lives, we realize

MIC CHECK—IS THIS THING ON?

that not only did God lay lessons before us but that even in our darkest hours, He was with us.

Don't stay mad, get glad, y'all, 'cause there is so much joy in finding the Lord's lessons in everyday life!

Can I Get an Amen?

Tamu and Zandra

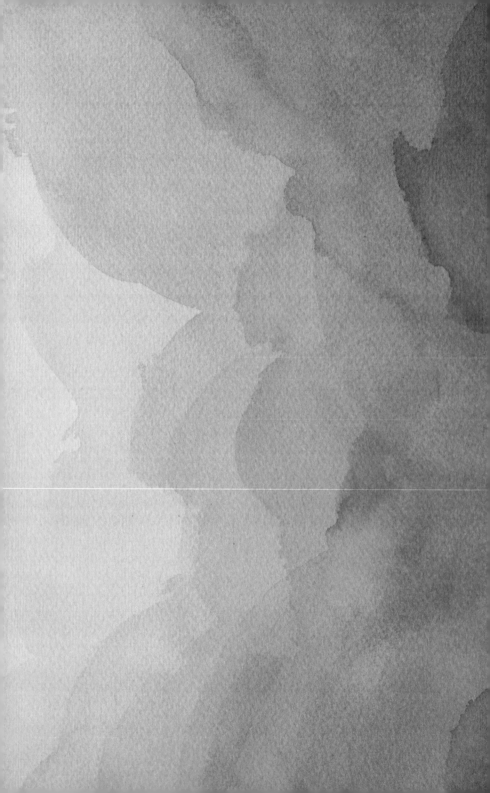

CHAPTER 1

BREAKING AND ENTERING

> They say when God closes a door, He opens a window. The key to finding the Lord's lessons is knowing that sometimes you gotta pick the lock.

FINDING JESUS IN JAIL

Jesus is not a criminal, but do you ever wonder why He spends so much time behind bars? Practically every inmate claims that he or she found Jesus in jail. Shoot, they got folks watching episodes of *Cops* and *Lockup Raw* hoping to catch a glimpse of Jesus. Where we come from, if you ask a kid how church was, they might reply, "It was real good—the Spirit was so strong today—but Jesus couldn't make it this morning. I think He was at the state pen. I don't know for sure, but my uncle said he found Him there one time."

We used to wonder why Jesus was always locked up, but not anymore, 'cause we found Jesus in jail too. Go on ahead and judge us if you want, but it's true. Our bars were invisible, yet they still seemed invincible. For some of us, sometimes life gets rough enough that it feels like we're doing hard time. Each of us with a personal prison of our own, serving separate sentences, but still the same Savior.

CAN I GET AN AMEN?

What we've learned is that you can put yourself in lockup, but God never throws away the key. Ask. Seek. Knock. He'll unlock the lessons.

  Can I Get an Amen?

  Tamu and Zandra

BACKGROUND CHECK

  Everybody has a record. It might not be the kind you can pull at the courthouse, but trust us, we all have one. In life, when we catch a case,* instead of claiming it got us on some trumped-up charges, what we need to do is work with Jesus to get our records expunged. The very first step in cleaning your record is running a check, 'cause you have to know what's dirty before you know what to clean. Our diaries are records that provide us with the data necessary to run a background check on ourselves. In diaries and journals we record our experiences, thoughts, feelings, emotions, and commentary on our life. They document our highs and, for some of us more often, our lows.

> *✱ A court case resulting from being charged with an alleged crime.*

4

BREAKING AND ENTERING

Even when we don't keep a physical diary, our memories can serve as records. We know what has transpired in our lives, especially those significant experiences that have become engraved in our minds and have seeped into our souls.

At some point in our lives, most of us will have a background or credit check run on us. People will run a check on you for just about anything these days: car loan, a job with benefits, housing, student loans, payday loans, or six months same as cash. And some folks will take it to a whole 'nother level: they check your Twitter, Facebook, and that old MySpace page you forgot about. Today a girl doesn't need your fingerprints to get your history. Y'all know what we're talking about. People want to get all up in the details of your past before they will deal with you in the present or the future. Why is that? Because for them our past tells a story, a story of who we might be.

See, that's the thing. When somebody is making a determination about us by using our background or credit history, they are judging us on our past and deciding whether or not that history tells the truth about us. Is it correct and indicative of who we are today? Sometimes it's correct, but other times it's wrong. A credit check can't tell you the details behind a single mother who missed paying on her car note because she was struggling to keep food on the table. A background check doesn't tell you that the addict with a criminal history has been a recovering addict for years. Why? Because when the world runs a check on you, it is based on your name, date of birth, and Social Security number and doesn't have a thing to do with Jesus.

Have you ever seen a background check that says, "On June 7, 2011, she accepted Jesus Christ as her personal Savior"? What about one that says, "On February 19, 1998, he backslid and didn't know how to find Jesus on the mainline to tell Him what he wants?" How about the mighty miracles God is working in your life? Do they show up on the world's background check? We've both held positions where we had access to background records, and we can tell you. The answer is no.

Can I Get an Amen?

Tamu and Zandra

LIAR, LIAR

From Zandra's Diary:

Today I told my first lie. Okay, it's probably not my first lie, but it's my first big one. My family decided to move back to the States from Trinidad and Tobago, and my father and I came ahead of everyone else to find work and housing. I'm only five, so I can't have a job . . . in America. My mother says you don't send your husband off to another country for an indefinite period of time by himself. You should send a kid with him because then they are less likely to get into trouble.

I started kindergarten, which I'm excited about, but if you could see how I look these days with my father trying to comb my hair! You'd think I was an orphan. I had one braid sticking straight out the top of my head and another coming straight out the side of my head. It was a hot mess.

Today this girl walked up to me and said, "Where's your mom? I never see you with your mom." I told her to mind her own business, but she wouldn't let it go. Before the words hit my mouth I knew I shouldn't say them, but I did anyway.

"She's dead," I said.

It did the trick; it shut Little Miss Busybody right up. Not for long, though. She made it her mission to act as the kindergarten version of the *National Enquirer* and spread the news. Hot off the press. I saw her bound from desk to desk, and then I would see the other child's eyes get large, and then they would both look over at me.

To me this seemed like a perfect solution. Now no kid would ask me where my mother was ever again. Hopefully, it would stop all of the questions: "Why don't your clothes match?" (Another side effect of my father dressing me.) "Why does your hair look like that?"

I was giving myself a mental pat on the back for my ingenuity when I saw Little Miss Busybody head up to our teacher's desk. As she leaned over and whispered into my teacher's ear, I felt my stomach flip-flop.

The next thing I know, they were looking at me. Then Miss Busybody starts pointing at me. As I saw the teacher motion for her to go to her seat, I tried to make myself invisible. I focused my eyes on my assignment, but I could tell from the way the hairs on the back of my neck were standing up that my teacher was trying to get my attention. My five-year-old mind reasoned that if I couldn't see her, maybe she couldn't see me.

I was wrong. As I heard the teacher call my name, I knew instantly I had no superpowers and had not become invisible. My teacher asked me to come to her desk. Though it was a few feet, I felt like I was walking the plank.

"Your classmate just told me that your mother is dead. That's not true, is it?"

Now my teacher would know I was a liar and then she would ask me why I lied, and I hated questions. It was other people's questions that had turned me into a liar in the first place.

My eyes began to fill with tears at the thought of what lay ahead, and I looked up into my teacher's brown eyes with my teary eyes. "Yes, it's true."

That was it. I had sealed my fate. I was going to hell, but forget the handbasket. Handbaskets weren't for little girls who looked at their kind teacher—the one who read stories to them on the story-time mat and let them take naps—right in the eye and told barefaced lies. I was probably going to hell on the wrong side of a pincushion. It would be something very prickly, for sure. I had told another lie to cover up my first lie.

Suddenly, my teacher grabbed me and snuggled me close to her bosom. "You poor baby," she said.

As I was engulfed in my teacher's warm embrace and the smell of her sweet perfume, I didn't feel so warm or so sweet, and that made me cry even more. My teacher dried my tears and moved my desk next to hers for the rest of the day. She gave our class a special talk about how every family is different. Some people have a mom, and some people don't, but we should be sensitive and nice to each other and not ask too many questions.

As I got special treatment from my teacher and my fellow classmates for having a dead mother, I felt rotten. At first. As the day progressed and Little Miss Busybody drew me a picture and everyone was being so nice to me, I began to think, "Hey, lying isn't so bad. Look at all the amazing perks I am getting." Kids were being nice to me, and my teacher was coddling me. What if "liar, liar, pants on fire" was a compliment?

As the weeks went on, it didn't seem like anyone would ever find out my lie. I felt safe and sound. Then it happened—a little something called parent-teacher conferences. I attended with my father, since there was no one to watch me because my very much alive mother was across the ocean. It started off great. My teacher sang my praises: I was doing well; I listened well; I played well with others. My father could not have been more proud.

As the meeting wrapped up, we stood up, and then my teacher said, "You are doing a great job with her. It must be so hard to raise a daughter without a mother."

My father looked at her, confused.

I grabbed his hand and tried to pull him out of the room.

"She has a mother," he said.

"I know," said my teacher. "I meant since her mother passed away."

I was pulling with all my might now, but the man wouldn't budge. He just stood there, looking confused, and she just stood there, looking so kind.

"Her mother is not dead," he said. "She's in another country."

Now it was my teacher's turn to look confused. As they began to sit back down, I became frantic. Why were they sitting? Why weren't we leaving? My lie was crumbling, and I would have to face it all.

As my teacher explained to my father how I had told her that my mother had died, he looked at me incredulously. I knew I was going to get it. My teacher suggested that she and my father talk alone, so they sent me into the hall.

The wait felt like an eternity. I was trying to imagine my fate. I would probably get sent to a school for liars, or worse, to jail. I knew I wouldn't survive jail. I had seen a movie once I wasn't supposed to be watching, and the women were in jail, and let's just say it wasn't pretty.

When they opened the door and asked me to come back in, my father began to lovingly explain to me that my mother was in another country and that she was alive. My teacher told me that even though I couldn't see my mother, it didn't mean that I didn't have a mother anymore.

This was worse than being a liar. My father and my teacher thought I was stupid! They thought that *I* really thought my mother was dead.

"I know my mother isn't dead," I said.

"Good, good," they said to me in slow speech like you use with a baby.

That night an expensive overseas call to my mother was made. By the time my father called me to the phone, he had already explained everything to her. I took the phone and said, "Hello."

My mother was in tears. "I'm not dead. I'm right here." She began to tell me how much she loved me and how she never would have sent me to the United States without her if it meant I thought she had died.

Great. Now my mother thought I was dumb as a box of rocks too.

The next day, while sitting in the office of the school counselor (that's where they send little girls who don't know the difference between out of the country and dead) to discuss my nonexistent abandonment issues, I realized two things. One, lying is a very bad idea. Once you lie, it takes more and more lies to cover up your original lie, and it could lead to people thinking that you are a little slow. And two, for a little girl who doesn't like to be asked questions, the counselor's office is not the place to be.

"Liar, liar, pants on fire" is not a compliment.

Not Living a Lie,

Zandra

CHECK YO'SELF BEFORE YOU WRECK YO'SELF*

Usually we don't write in our diaries one day and then read what we wrote the next. Some time usually elapses between when we record and when we look back. But we should evaluate our lives regularly and be performing spiritual background checks on ourselves.

> * You better reevaluate your actions before you get yourself into serious trouble.

Spiritual background checks can give us a wealth of information. And unlike the world's background check, this history shows so much more. It shows change, growth, where we have gone off the beaten path, how we got where we are today, and even how we can get where we need to be tomorrow. More importantly, it shows us how the Lord has been working in our lives and what He is trying to teach us.

In real life, nobody has a clean record. We all have made mistakes, we all have struggles in our lives, but like they say, "The struggles make us stronger, but changes make us wiser." God puts things in our path not just to strengthen us but to help us learn from them and choose to change to become more like our Savior.

Some of us may have an aversion to running a background check on ourselves. Shoot, it's daunting enough when the world runs one on us. Believe us, we have wondered why anybody needs to know all our business like that. Bosses are so nosey! Our spiritual history shows us the blemishes on our records so that we can have the opportunity to clean them up. With the world's background check, our errors are there, usually forever. Even when we change, they are still available for viewing. But because of a loving Savior, we can change direction and be forgiven. Our history will now record our good.

In life we should look for the lessons and acknowledge the blessings. There are times when our actions force us to repeat a lesson, but we have the ability to look back, jog our memory, and brush up on the course. When we don't learn from our experiences, we keep repeating the negative. We often acknowledge the good things, but then we carry the negative in a more prominent place in our life.

We must be willing to look at our lives and be honest about what we find there. "Trust in the Lord with all thine heart; and lean not unto thine own understanding. In all thy ways acknowledge him, and he shall direct thy paths" (Proverbs 3:5–6).

As we've looked back in our diaries, we've encountered the hopelessness and the fear that we recorded while going through our dark moments, and we were able to realize that where we are now is so different from where we were then. In times when we didn't think we could go on, suddenly there we were living, breathing, and experiencing moments of joy. What had changed? What was different in our lives? What did we know now that we didn't know then? Who had delivered us?

As we recognized the lessons, the triumphs, the changes of heart, and God's hands in our lives, we realized that our diaries weren't just a record of trials and tribulations. They were books of blessings. Today we can see how the Lord was with us in times when we didn't even think He was there. Like they say where we're from, "Check yo'self before you wreck yo'self."

Can I Get an Amen?

Tamu and Zandra

BOUNCED CHECK

When we first set out to utilize the power of a spiritual background check, it can be hard. Like we said, digging into the past isn't always easy, but once we see the benefits and reap the blessings, some of us get real excited about running background checks. Maybe a little too excited. Now what we need err'body to know is that spiritual background checks are a personal thing. Just because you have the key that unlocks your spiritual truths doesn't give you license to be pickin' other folks' locks. Don't get so excited about your background check that now you are try'na run checks on everybody else. You can't start reading other people's diaries trying to find their lessons when you just barely found your own. Jesus did not assign you to a special ops task force and ask you to start checkin' everybody else. Remember, you are your brother's keeper, not your brother's creeper, ummkay?

BREAKING AND ENTERING

Hardly anybody writes checks these days, but most of us know what a bounced check is. Shoot, where some of us come from, we thought there were only two types of checks: paychecks and bounced checks. It was like a whole new world when we found out that not all checks bounced. We're 'bout to give y'all a little spiritual finance lesson up in here. The reason that a check bounces is that there are insufficient funds in the bank that the check is written on for the check to clear. That's basically how running a spiritual background check on your mama, daddy, cousin, neighbor, and anybody else works. It's gon' bounce, boo,* because concerning them, you have insufficient information. We don't have time to be all up in anybody else's background, because even when we unlock the lessons in our own, trust us, there's plenty more where that came from.

> ✱ Term of endearment for a loved one.

Can I Get an Amen?

Tamu and Zandra

SLIPPERY SLOPE

From Tamu's Diary:

I don't know why I got into my uncle's car without my shoes on, but I did. My mother was constantly on my case for going outside with only my footsies on. (Don't act like you didn't used to sport ankle socks with a colorful little ball on the back. If you didn't have a pair, you should have.) We were picking up a few odds and ends for my mother's birthday party. My uncle was driving, and I was in the backseat with my little sister and Terrance. I had a huge crush on him, but he thought of me as a kid sister.

When we pulled into the store parking lot, my little sister noticed that I didn't have on my shoes and said, "Ohhh, you are bold! Mama is going to kill you!"

I reminded my sister that snitches get stitches and end up in ditches.

"Just kidding," she smiled.

It started to drizzle as we walked into the store. I hoped that by the time we finished shopping, the weather would pass. But that's not how it happened for me; Mother Nature was not on my time clock. There was a burst of thunder, and then it started pouring rain. I'd taken my barefooted behind to the store and got caught up in a rainstorm. So I did what any normal person in that situation would have done. I walked to the shoe department and looked for a pair of slippers to "borrow." I just needed something to keep my feet dry and my socks from getting muddy. So I slipped on a pair of fuzzy pink slippers. I knew it was wrong, but I had a plan. I was going to "borrow" the slippers and pay the store back when my funds came in. I didn't have a job at the time, but I was working on it.

My little sister saw what I was doing, took off the shoes she wore into the store, and slipped on a pair of pink fuzzy slippers too. I asked her what she was doing.

She looked at me and said, "You got a new pair of slippers, and I want a pair too."

"What are you going to do with your old shoes?" I asked her.

She threw them behind the shoe rack. I thought about telling her that stealing was wrong and that she didn't need the slippers, but what could I say? I was stealing, and she had seen me do it. Plus, I always hated it when adults said things like, "Do as I say, not as I do!" The only way to get my sister to take off her slippers was for me to take off my slippers, and I wasn't going to do that.

"Mama is going to kill you if you leave your shoes here."

She shrugged, and we ran to find my uncle and Terrance. The two of them had no idea that we were stealing and they would be harboring criminals.

Our shopping was complete, and we had started to leave the store when two men approached us. One was a short, stout man; the other was a beautiful, slender, chocolate brotha with an athletic build. They both were security guards. As we got to the door, the brotha said, "Excuse me. Can I talk to you two young ladies?"

Before we could say anything, my uncle said, "They're with me, man. What do you need to say to them?"

I was panicking. I wanted to die. What was I going to do?

One security guard grabbed my arm, and the other guard reached for my little sister.

Before anyone could say anything, Terrance hit the brotha in the face and shouted, "Get your hands off my sister!"

The automatic doors opened just then, and everyone except my uncle ran. We ran past the cars and through the parking lot to the six-lane street. I slowed down to run at a pace my sister could keep up with. Terrance got to the median and yelled for us to hurry up, as two store workers plus the security guards ran after us. My sister froze as the workers got closer. I saved myself and left my sister on the side of the road as I ran across three lanes to the island in the middle. Traffic was heavy, and that separated me from the search party.

Terrance was now completely across the street, yelling for me to hurry up.

I looked back and saw my sister get snatched up. Tears rolling down her face, she was yelling, "Please don't leave me."

I had to go back to her. I waited for traffic to clear and slowly (as slow as a person crossing a busy street could) walked back to where my sister was standing with the store workers and security guards. During my walk of shame back into the store, I saw a couple of kids from my school. I felt humiliated and embarrassed.

The security guard that Terrance hit in the face was heated! He said that what we did was no longer considered petty theft. It was now robbery and assault, and since I was the oldest, I would be charged. I grew up watching shows like *CHiPs, Cagney and Lacey,* and *Dukes of Hazzard,* so I knew you had to be tough when dealing with the po-po* in order to get a better deal. They kept asking us "if" we'd stolen the slippers, which in my mind meant they weren't 100 percent

* The police.

sure we had. I had the typical television criminal attitude, which didn't do me any good. I kept insisting that we had the slippers on when we came into the store and that the undercover guy must have seen me adjusting my slippers. They couldn't figure out what we had done with the shoes we had on when we entered the store, because they couldn't imagine that we had entered the store, as dressed up as we were, without any shoes on. Yes, I was shoplifting in a church dress. (Don't judge me!)

The frustrated store manager was about to turn us loose when one of the security guys got creative. "Before we let you go, we want to go over our in-store footage." He pointed to a monitor and said, "If we find that you are lying to us, you're going to jail, and your parents are going to be fined five thousand dollars for each pair of stolen slippers!"

He should just have called Child Protective Services right then, because I would need protection! My mama had a fit if I didn't return library books on time because she didn't appreciate paying avoidable fines. Now this brotha was telling me that my mama was going to have to pay ten thousand dollars because my sister and I had decided to steal some five-dollar slippers.

BREAKING AND ENTERING

Even though my body had a physical reaction to what he was telling us, my mouth would not yield. My sister started crying and asked me if we could just tell the truth. The look I shot her said it all, and she zipped her lips like a tight dress on a fat kid. But it was too late; the security guard had heard her. They asked my sister to go with them into a different room. I squeezed her hand, which meant, "Don't say NOTHING!" She nodded to let me know she knew what the squeeze meant.

That girl wasn't even in that room five minutes before they came back and told me everything. When I say everything, I mean err'thang! What we had for breakfast, what we talked about in the car, the conversation we had when we slipped on those ugly Pepto-pink fuzzy slippers!

There was a knock on the door, and I heard my mother say, "I'm Susie. I believe you have my children in there with you."

The door opened, and my mama was standing right there, looking like both friend and foe. Her tone was very calm and cool when she spoke to them, but when she spoke to me her tone was completely different. "Wait 'til you get home!" How did she do that? When she was speaking to them it was all honey, but with me it was all vinegar.

Now I actually wanted to go to jail, anywhere except home with my mama! Mama put her face as close to mine as she could without head-butting me and said, "Have you completely lost your mind?"

I wasn't new to this question or questions of the type, either. Some questions aren't meant to be answered, not out loud anyway. The police, who arrived shortly after my mother, stood there letting my mama do their job of questioning me.

With a chuckle, one of the officers said, "Just so we're clear, when ya mama beats your butt, we are all just going to sit here. We might even laugh, 'cause you need to get whooped."

What? Didn't they know those words were like giving an alcoholic permission to drink a glass of wine? My mama didn't need his permission to discipline me! She wouldn't care if the police were there or not, so I certainly didn't need anyone giving suggestions. "Yeah, we got a store full of belts that we can donate to her to use today and anytime in the future."

"Ain't it amazing how agreeable kids get when their parents show up?" I heard another of the security guards say. "That's how you can tell which kids come from a good home with parents that care, and which kids don't. This lady knows her kids, and she cares about them." Well, right now I wanted to be one of those kids whose parents didn't care.

On television shows there is always a good cop and a bad cop, but now that my mama was playing both roles and my little sister had already cut a deal by telling the truth, I knew there would be no deal for me. The jig was up. I confessed to stealing the pink slippers. I told them how I did it, but I didn't tell them the name of the guy who had run from the security guard. My mama kept asking me who was with us. Terrance was over eighteen, and they were talking about sending him to jail. I didn't want that to happen to him, not for trying to protect my sister and me.

Eventually I was issued a ticket and told that I was not allowed to shop at that store again unless I was with my mother. The security guard told us that we were caught stealing because he had noticed how nicely and put together we were dressed. He said that just as he noticed that I was a beautiful young lady, I ripped the tag off the slippers and put them on my feet. "I thought I'd share that with you before you left, because you never know when someone is noticing you."

I could tell that my mama was embarrassed. She apologized to the security guards. She made me apologize to them too, and I did. She explained that she was just as shocked as he was, and she'd never had a problem like this from me. Then she said something that I will never forget: "She's a Mormon, and Mormons aren't supposed to steal."

Looking into my mother's eyes, I could tell she felt embarrassed and heavy hearted. The police officer said he would never in a million years have guessed I was a Latter-day Saint. That made me feel even worse.

"She even goes to early morning seminary," my mother told them.

I don't know why I kept trying to act so tough, because I wasn't. I tried not to cry, but trying did nothing to stop the tears from falling. The officer, the store manager, and the security guards were all staring at me. I didn't know what to say, and I didn't think it was a good time to offer them a Book of Mormon. The only thing left to do was apologize to everyone. I kept my head down and stared at the floor.

Noticing that they had hit a soft spot, the officer said, "The good thing about this is that you got caught. There are a lot of people who go on stealing for years, and by the time they get caught, they are adults and it's difficult to stop. You have a community of people around you that want to help you put an end to this. I don't ever want to see you in this type of situation again. Do you understand me?"

I nodded.

He patted me on my back and said to everyone else in the room, "This one is going to be all right. She is trying to be tough, but she has a soft heart, I can tell." With that they released my sister and me into my mother's custody.

I guess the officer didn't like me enough to put me in a detention center, so I didn't have any choice but to go home with my mama. As soon as we got in the car, my mother looked at me and told me how I had humiliated her, the family, the community, the Church—and all on her birthday.

"I have a house full of people, and I had to come down here and rescue your li'l thieving behind," she said.

I wanted to jump out of the car. I had forgotten that my aunts, uncles, and cousins were all at my house waiting to celebrate my mother's birthday. As Mr. Needham, one of my teachers, would tell us, "Make a decision, see it through, and suffer the consequences." There were consequences to suffer, all right, and I knew my mother would make me see my way through them. My parents chastised me and reminded me that I could have been arrested, put on probation, fined, or all of the above. All of which were good reasons not to steal. The thing that had the most effect on me, however, was realizing that my choices had a ripple effect on the communities that I belonged to. I also realized that my little sister looked up to me and that I shouldn't do anything that I didn't want her or any of the rest of my siblings doing. Until that day, I thought my choices affected only me. I didn't realize that people would judge not only me but the communities that I was a part of as well.

Remorsefully,

Tamu

HIDE 'N SEEK

Finding the Lord's lessons is twofold. We can find them in the past, and we can find them in the present. And we should seek them in both places. While our spiritual background check is important, it is just that, a check. It's similar to driving a car. We are taught to check the rearview mirror but always return our attention to the road.

So yes, we may need to look back in time, but we don't stay there. We should always return our gaze to the present and keep our focus on our Father in Heaven because biblical history shows that looking back can sometimes get you turned into a pillar of salt. Nobody wants to kick it with a salty person.

We don't have to wait until our moments become history to find what the Lord is trying to teach us. The scriptures tell us, "But if from thence thou shalt seek the Lord thy God, thou shalt find him, if thou seek him with all thy heart and with all thy soul" (Deuteronomy 4:29). Too many times we focus on the finish line of our trial and forget to yield to the voice of the coach. He tells us in Psalms to cast our burdens upon him (Psalm 55:22). Everybody should know how to play hide 'n seek, but just in case you don't, the premise is that everybody hides, and then one person sets off to find them. And true to the game, life is the same: If we seek God's lessons, we are bound to find the hidden gems.

"Seek good, and not evil, that ye may live: and so the Lord, the God of hosts, shall be with you, as ye have spoken" (Amos 5:14). In *all* that we do, are we seeking good and shunning evil? When you are on Twitter, do you seek good? Technology is a beautiful thing. A couple of years ago, we didn't even know who Siri was, but today she is our homegirl. It's sometimes hard for us to remember how we used to get anywhere before Siri was giving us driving directions. How did we ever pick a restaurant without Siri's help? As we use technology, social media, print media, and even reality TV, we have to make a conscious choice to seek good, and not evil. You can find the most uplifting sermons online, but guess what? You can find pornography there, too.

Look, y'all, God is up on game. He stays with the times, and He will teach us where He can reach us and always in a language we can understand. God can keep up with you while you are keeping up with the Kardashians, He can show His face on Facebook, and He can put His praise on Pinterest, but we won't find the lessons unless we seek good and not evil.

Can I Get an Amen?

Tamu and Zandra

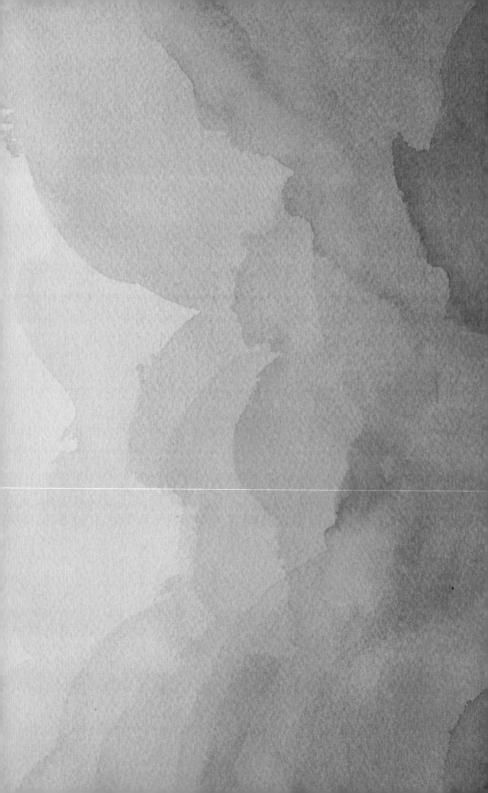

CHAPTER 2

STAND

> Life is not a sit-down job.
> Well, unless you're Rosa Parks,
> but in her case sitting down was
> actually standing up.

SET YOUR STANDARDS HIGH SO YOU CAN FLY

When people start thinking of standards, they automatically start naming all the things that somebody else is telling them they can't do. Christian values often come under fire for being too confining and old-fashioned. People have asked us, "Don't you want to live your life in freedom?" That question always shocks us. Simply put, Christian values are the teachings of Jesus. Our question back to them is, "How has following Jesus ever imprisoned anyone?" Except for Daniel, okay, well, and maybe a few other people, but who's getting thrown into a lion's den these days?

We've never felt restricted by following the Savior. Quite the opposite. For us there is freedom in maintaining positive values. The Ten Commandments are often thought of as a list of don'ts, but we see them as a list of freedoms. "Thou shalt not steal" (even a pair of fuzzy pink slippers) means we are free to remain on the right side of jail bars. We are free to earn the respect of our peers because we respect their property. "Thou shalt not commit adultery" means that we are free to foster happy, healthy, and loving marriages. "Thou shalt not bear false witness" means that we can let the truth set us free.

All of us have values that affect the standards we put in place in our lives. For us, the teachings of Christ have played a tremendous part in developing ours.

Can I Get an Amen?

Tamu and Zandra

SUSIE SET THE STANDARD

From Tamu's Diary:

My mama used to make me practice saying NO!!! I want you to recognize that NO!!! is in all caps with not one, not two, but three exclamation points because that is how she had me say it. It wasn't no; it was "NO!!!" My mama took stranger danger to a whole 'nother level. It wasn't just about saying no to the man in the kidnapper van who wants you to come help him find his lost puppy, or saying no to drugs. It was about saying NO!!! to everything.

I was probably in the first grade when Mama let me know that I would be saying NO!!! when my friends and I turned sixteen and they got their brand-new-to-them used cars and offered me a ride. I turned sixteen when a sweet sixteen was still a sweet sixteen. Now there are super-sweet sixteens, and the MTV cameras are there filming these elaborate parties and kids are getting diamonds and Bentleys and parents are paying Justin Beiber hundreds of thousands of dollars to show up for five minutes and sing. No, boo, nobody was doing all that when I turned sixteen.

I knew I couldn't accept rides from teenage drivers because my mama had already made me practice telling them NO!!! so many times starting at age six that by the time I was finally offered a ride by one of my friends, my response was, "Naw, I'm cool," before I even realized it. By the time I was sixteen, I had realized that saying NO!!! makes your friends look at you crazy. (I toned it down a little, but to this day I will still say NO!!! to anyone trying to get me into a large van with dark tinted windows.)

So here's exactly what happened to me one day while waiting for the bus with some of my friends. Our friend

Jackie pulled up and asked us if we wanted a ride, so as I was programmed to do, I said "NO!!!" My other friends looked at me like I had lost my mind. They left me standing at the bus stop alone as they jumped in Jackie's hooptie* and rolled out. I stood there alone, feeling bamboozled, as I waited for the bus. Why did I say no? I felt like an idiot. I hadn't even given it a first thought, never mind a second one.

Then it dawned on me. My mama did this to me! I began to think she really did have me programmed. Maybe she had placed a chip in my head, or worse, maybe a rule that had been put in place by my mama had subconsciously become a standard that I had decided I would abide by in my own life. Well, that was it! In that instant I decided I was going to slough off that standard. The next time Jackie offered me a ride, I was taking it. No more public transportation for me. All my friends were getting home nearly an hour and a half before me, and my social life was suffering while I waited for the city bus. My mama was ruining my life.

It was my freshman year of high school, and my family had moved from San Bernardino to Fresno. I mean, who moves from Southern California to Central California? Old

> * A car that might not look the best but will get you where you need to go.

folks, that's who. Had my parents even bothered to ask me if I wanted to move? Absolutely not, because with all that NO!!! I had been programmed to recite, it surely would have been my answer. NO!!! I didn't want to leave all my friends behind, go to a new school without any of my cousins, and start all over in Fresno. My freshman year had been ruined, and just when it seemed like it might begin to get a little bit better, it crumbled before my very eyes as I waited friendless for FAX (Fresno Area Express) to pick me up.

One day soon after I made the decision to break the rule of not driving with teenage drivers, the phone rang. I heard my mama answer it, and a few moments later I heard my mama crying. Actually, she wasn't really crying. She was doing that black-mama holler-yell-cry, you know what I mean. The type of cry you can feel in your soul. Some call it a pain cry, the kind where you almost pass out.

"Oh no, Jesus, Lawd, not all of 'em, Jesus! No!" Now my mama had my full attention. I knew that cry immediately. Someone had died. My heart felt like it was going to pop out of my chest. I wanted to know who had died, but I *didn't* want to know who had died. I listened on. I heard lots of someones had died, but who? Then came the tears, lots of tears. As the tears poured down Mama's face, Daddy took the phone.

Daddy began to get details. "Yeah. Oh naw, that is too bad." He tried to retain a manly composure, but I could see the concern and pain written across his face. Then his eyes began to water. He was trying to remain strong for my mama, but something in the way he looked at me made me think he might be trying to remain strong for me, too.

"Susie-Mae, c'mon now," he said. "We gotta be strong for the girl."

He motioned for me to come over to him. My tears started to stream before he even said anything more to me because I knew whatever he was about to say was going to end with so-and-so is dead. The angel of death was no stranger to our home. I was crying, Mama was sobbing, and Daddy's voice was beginning to crack. I stood there in awe as he explained that my friends back home in Southern California—Dorian, Darron, Tammy, and Keysha—had been in a car accident. Dorian had gotten a brand-new car for his sixteenth birthday, and he and the others were going to lunch when he turned a corner too fast and lost control of the vehicle. Three of my four friends had been killed. Only Keysha had survived but not without trauma and lasting emotional scars. My own life too had gotten real—again.

I felt helpless. I was hundreds of miles away in Fresno. This was before cell phones, texting, and Facebook. We did have pagers back then. But who was I going to page, and even if I did page someone, who was going to call me back? Long distance meant something back then; it meant I had to wait a long time to make a call because it was just after five o'clock and the price break in long-distance phone rates didn't kick in until seven o'clock. As I sat there waiting for the short hand to reach the seven and the long hand to reach the twelve, I no longer felt programmed. I had clarity. My mama hadn't just taught me to say "NO!!!" She had taught me how to "live." I'd like to believe that if I hadn't moved and was still back in SoCal that when my friend Dorian offered me that ride to lunch, I would have said what my mother had me practicing since the age of six: "NO!!!"

Sometimes it's not only about standing for something or falling for something. Sometimes it's about making a decision before you are ever even put into a situation.

Just Say NO!!!

Tamu

LAST MAN STANDING

From Zandra's Diary:

I made the decision not to drink alcohol when I was around ten years old. Granny Louise, Aunty Carol, my cousin Stella, and I were out to dinner one night in New York. They said we could pick a fun drink, so my cousin, who was about fifteen years old at the time, and I decided to order piña coladas. I hadn't tasted mine yet, but my cousin appeared to be enjoying her drink so much that her mom decided to take a sip. I could see her eyebrows raise. Then she motioned for the waiter and asked him if the pina coladas were virgin. After checking with the bartender, the waiter returned with a worried look on his face. No, they weren't nonalcoholic. He apologized profusely and said he would be back with two fresh, legal-to-serve-to-a-minor coladas. He left the alcoholic drinks, on the house of course, for Aunty and Granny to enjoy.

Well, my cousin's drink was almost all gone, so her mom said she could go ahead and finish; this would be her once-a-year sip that she usually got for toasting around the holidays. Granny pushed my drink towards me and said I was allowed to have a few sips too. I put my hands around the glass and thought for a moment. Some people in my family drank alcohol and some people didn't, and in that moment I just made up my mind that I wouldn't try alcohol. "No, thanks," I said to Granny. She took the drink and sipped on it.

Once I made that decision, I never had to think about it again. If I'm offered a drink, I say, "No, thanks."

If they say, "Are you sure?" I say, "I don't drink."

As I got older, I maintained my standard of not drinking alcohol, and despite what some teenagers may think, it did not make me a loser in high school. It just made me the official designated driver. One weekend I attended a house party with some of my friends. As we stepped inside the house, I was handed the car keys, and my friends headed off to the cooler. The fact that the host's parents were out of town had drawn quite a crowd, and the supply of alcohol seemed endless. Whenever I attended a party as sober sista, my party experience was always the same. At the beginning of the party, I mingled, met people, danced, talked, and laughed. As the night progressed and my peers became more intoxicated, the energy of the party went wild. I won't detail all of that party's events, but I will say that I don't know how the piercing gun from the mall kiosk ended up at the party, but it did. And I don't know who thought they were qualified to use said piercing gun, but somebody did. And I can't for the life of me figure out why somebody would volunteer to be pierced, but they did. So you know I can't even understand why folks were trying to act shocked later when said piercings that were performed by a highly unqualified and inebriated teenager became infected, but they were. My philosophy is say no to drugs, drinking, and piercings at parties.

Eventually the party waned, and everyone began losing energy. Some people sat down, others passed out, and eventually I was the last man standing. As it is, when you are a teenaged designated driver, you look around at some point and realize you are the only one with your wits about you. Teenagers don't have good sense. They drink to get drunk, and that's why they shouldn't drink, because our brains aren't fully cooked until we're much older.

As I looked around at the mess and the people lying everywhere, I had a few thoughts. One, I really didn't understand what was so fun about being drunk. Two, Kyle was really going to be in trouble if he couldn't get that girl's throw-up out of his mom's expensive carpet. And three, I wondered if anyone here would care if I joined them in their prehangover misery. So I picked up an empty beer bottle from the counter and threw back my head like I was about to drain it. Before I could even get the rim of the bottle to my mouth, I felt the bottle being snatched from my hand.

"What the [bleep] do you thinking you're doing?" my friend Tanya yelled at me.

I don't know how she got into the kitchen so fast. She was so drunk that I had given up trying to have a coherent conversation with her just a few moments earlier.

A girl who was sleeping on the kitchen counter sat up and said to Tanya, "What's your problem? Give her back her beer."

"Shut up and mind your own business. She doesn't drink," said Tanya. "She's never had alcohol a day in her life."

"Never?" said Counter-Sleeper Girl.

I shook my head no.

"So you gonna try it?"

"She's not trying anything," said Tanya before I could even answer.

"What, are you her mother?" asked Counter-Sleeper Girl.

Tanya grabbed my hand and said quietly, "Why you wanna drink?"

"Well, everyone else is," I said.

"So what?" she said. "We're us, and you're you."

All of a sudden I just got the giggles.

"I don't know why you think this is funny," she said. She was still holding the beer bottle she had snatched from me.

"Shake it," I said, pointing to the bottle.

She looked confused but shook it anyway. As she realized it was empty, a look of relief came over her face.

"You scared me!" she said, playfully pushing me. "Feel my heart."

She placed my hand on her chest, and I felt her rapid heartbeat. "I really thought you were going to drink."

"Looks like you wouldn't have let me," I replied.

"Let's get out of here," Tanya said.

As we sat across from each other in the booth at the diner while she sobered up and I sipped a hot cocoa, I realized that even though we had different beliefs, Tanya respected mine and would hold me accountable for what I claimed I stood for. Those are the kind of friends a girl needs in her corner.

Your Sober Sista,

Zandra

GOD'S GOT YOUR BACK

Listen, life really isn't a sit-down job; it's a participation sport. It's all about action, and what we stand for is a big, big part of that. You wanna know why we said that when

Rosa Parks sat down, she was actually standing up? Because on December 1, 1955, when that bus driver told her to give up her seat and move to the back of the bus, she had a choice. You see, long before that moment, Ms. Parks had decided it was wrong for blacks to be treated unequally. At that moment, she could do as she was told and head back, or she could do exactly what she did, stay seated and stand up for what she knew was right.

God has equipped us with all the tools to live the happiest lives possible, but He doesn't force us to put them to use, and thankfully He doesn't expect us to be perfect. In fact, Jesus has made it possible for us to get back up every time we fall, and you can't tell us it doesn't make it a whole lot easier to stand knowing God's got your back.

Can I Get an Amen?

Tamu and Zandra

STANDING IN THE STREETLIGHT

From Zandra's Diary:

My parents have this thing about being in the house by the time the streetlights come on. Today I was chillin' with my friends when the streetlights flickered on. All the smart kids went home. I, on the other hand, stayed back with the kids whose parents didn't have a streetlight rule. I should have just taken my behind home because I couldn't even relax. You know that feeling where you keep turning around to see what's behind you, because at any moment you expect someone to roll up on you,* snatch you by the shirt collar, spin you around, and ask you if you've lost your mind? If you don't know that feeling, then either you never had a curfew or you were smart enough not to ignore your curfew.

By the time I heard my name being yelled from the porch, I was already sweating buckets. I said my good-byes to my friends and tried to be sincere, since it was very likely that this would be the last time they ever saw me. I couldn't walk because the last thing I wanted my mother to accuse me of was "strolling in" past curfew. For some folks, *stroll* is a perfectly fine word but not at my house. Some people take a stroll in the park but not me. I don't stroll anywhere. Had I been anything but running I would have heard, "Look at the hour," and I would have had nothing to look at because I was allowed to wear my watch only on special occasions and there was no clock on the front porch.

> ✲ Catch you off guard.

STAND

"I had to climb out of bed . . . " The way my mother said it, you would have thought my parents' bed was on the top of a mountain the way they were always climbing in and out of it. " . . . yell your name at the top of my lungs . . . " Is it possible to yell at the bottom of your lungs? " . . . and here you come strolling in like you don't have a care in the world."

When I reached the front porch, out of breath from running, I was of course asked if I had lost my mind, to which there is no real answer because it's not even a real question. Anything that comes out of your mouth after that can and will be used to prove that you indeed have lost your mind.

When my front porch trial came to an end, the verdict was that if I thought I was going to be traipsing in and out of the house whenever I pleased, I had another think coming because they were not going to stand for that. That night I learned there were things my folks were not going to stand for, and it got me wondering, what are the things I won't stand for?

Surprisingly Still Alive,

Zandra

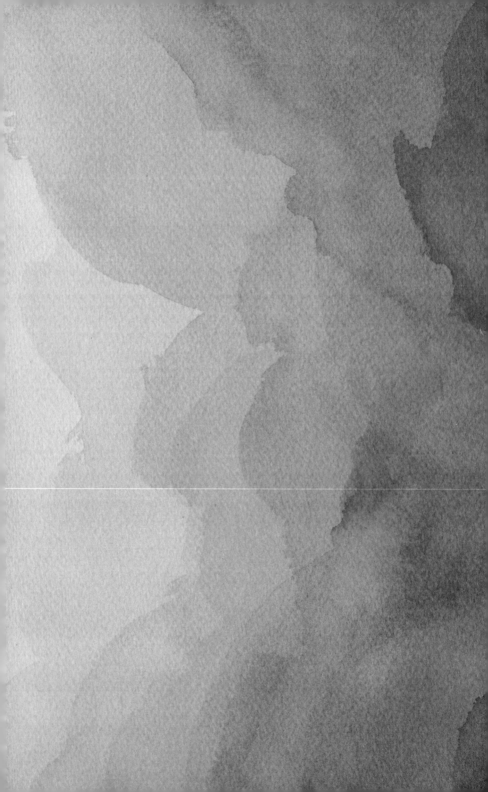

CHAPTER 3

FEAST OF FAITH

Sometimes you gotta start
a food fight to get through tribulation,
'cause God says we can throw
small mustard seeds at
big problems and
make 'em move.

GOT A LITTLE, GET A LOT

The word of God likens faith to a mustard seed: "If ye have faith as a grain of mustard seed, ye shall say unto this mountain, Remove hence to yonder place; and it shall remove; and nothing shall be impossible unto you" (Matthew 17:20).

That's a beautiful thing, and we're gonna tell you why. Have you ever seen a mustard seed? Well, it's so tiny it's teensy, but because God is great, He says that with small faith we can do big things! So how come it's sometimes hard for us to believe it, but when it's Vegas giving the odds, some folks are happy to pony up their small dollar on the hope of winning a million? Our best bet is with the Lord's lotto, where with just finite faith in His word, we can witness boundless blessings.

Can I Get an Amen?

Tamu and Zandra

THE FIRST FISH FRY

From Zandra's Diary:

When I was young, we often attended Sunday services in our own congregation and then went to church with Granny Louise, who was a member of a Baptist church. It did make for a very long Sunday, but I enjoyed attending church with my granny.

Even though she was not a Latter-day Saint, Granny was always at our church because she attended whenever we asked her to. If there was a Primary* program, she was there. If there was a baptism, she was there. If there was a ward** activity, she was there. Pretty much if we sneezed and we wanted her at church with us, she was there.

There were special Sundays at Granny's church when they had a dinner after the service. A fish fry. On those Sundays we could clap our hands, stomp our feet, praise the Lord, and then get something to eat! On that Sunday, you had better get there early if

* Children's Sunday School.

** A congregation; not to be confused with a ward in a mental institution, although some of the same people may be found at both.

you wanted a seat. The Lord had a packed house that day. I would look around the chapel at all the people stuffed in the pews and think, "I hope the church ladies cooked enough, because I sure am hungry."

The choir was always good at Granny's church, but on fish fry Sunday, it was exceptional. The preacher was of course a little long winded. He probably figured he needed to hit the Lord's message home for those in the congregation that wouldn't be coming back until next year's fish fry. As soon as the preacher said amen, everyone would make a mad dash outside. I would stand there in line with my plate, thinking, "Oh, I hope I make it up there before all of Granny's greens are gone."

When I finally reached the table, spread with a variety of wonderful foods, a church lady named something like Miss Mildred would take my plate and begin to serve me. Then I would have to tell her, "Miss Mildred, could I have the greens from that pot over there?"

And she'd say, "They're all the same. Greens are greens."

And of course she knew that was a lie, because we all knew about the pot of greens from the really nice church lady who couldn't cook but always wanted to provide something. They kept it in the kitchen, and everyone prayed that we wouldn't run out of greens and have to bring out her pot.

"Please?" I'd say. "My granny made the ones in that pot."

She'd act like she was miffed about it, but then she'd give me a scoop of them.

"Just a little more, please, Miss Mildred," I'd say, after I saw how tiny the scoop was.

"Look here. We've got a lot of people to serve," she'd tell me.

Then somebody would pass by, maybe the preacher, and he'd say, "Come on now, Sister Mildred, if Jesus could feed five thousand with five loaves and two fishes, then I'm sure we'll be all right . . . Give the baby a little more greens."

Then Miss Mildred would smile at the preacher and give me a good-sized helping.

After the preacher left, she would look at me and say, "All right now. You got plenty of greens. I better not see you up here asking for seconds."

I'd take my plateful of food to the table where my family was sitting and look around. Everyone was happy and smiling, and everyone was fed—all those people, and everyone got a plate. Then I would wonder if that was what it was like when Jesus fed the five thousand. Maybe Jesus looked around and saw everyone was happy and smiling and well fed. As I would take a bite of that delicious, golden, crispy fish, and it melted in my mouth, I'd imagine that as good as this fish tasted, Jesus's must've been even more divine. Boy, I would love to have been at Jesus's fish fry!

Of course Granny loved us, but I think much of her willingness to attend church with us was because my parents allowed her grandchildren to attend church with her also. Now that Granny has gone to glory, I cannot express how grateful I am for those extra-long Sundays. They are precious memories that I cherish, memories centered on Christ. I don't see many fish fry Sundays these days, but I'm still well fed. You see, when you feast on the Savior's word, you are always full. Everyone can partake; there is plenty to go around at the Lord's table. It was an absolute miracle when Jesus fed five thousand with just five loaves of bread and two fishes, and if we let Him, He can feed us all too, including the entire world. That's billions of people! Oh, what a fish fry that would be!

Feasting upon the Word,

Zandra

AIN'T NOBODY DRINKIN' THAT KOOL-AID

From Tamu's Diary:

I don't know why there are so many nosey people in my life. People, not just family and close friends but random people in this neighborhood, are up in arms because me, Mama, and Daddy joined The Church of Jesus Christ of Latter-day Saints.

My friend Erma was in town visiting her grandmother. Usually when she was in town, we would catch up on school, movies, boys, and all the latest trends (maybe not in that order, but you get the picture). She was at my house telling me all about the drama at her school and drinking Kool-Aid when out of the blue she asked me if we'd put anything special in her Kool-Aid. She said that her grandmother told her not to eat or drink anything at my house because we had joined a cult. I didn't even know what a cult was, but I knew it was probably not a good thing because of the way she said it.

She also said that her grandmother told her that we didn't read the Bible. When I told her that we did read the Bible, Erma wanted to see it. The missionaries had given my parents and me new scriptures right before we got baptized. I went and got my Bible. Erma inspected it like she was a detective. It was the King James Version. She asked me how I got my name on it. I didn't know how they got my name on it, because it was a gift. It must have passed her approval because she finished drinking her Kool-Aid and we finished talking about the drama at school.

I thought we were cool until Erma came to my house the next day, banging on my door like she had a search warrant. Not only did she accuse me of lying to her about my Bible but she accused my parents, my church, and me of all kinds of crazy stuff. She called the Church a cult and claimed they had just started letting black people join it. She said that my father only joined the Church because he wanted to take on other wives, and the "Mormon cult" encourages men to marry a whole lot of women.

Her mouth was running like diarrhea; she wasn't letting me get a word in. To add insult to injury, she had the nerve to accuse me of putting a "cult–joining drug" into her Kool-Aid. She claimed the Kool-Aid I had given her the day before had made her sick.

Now, even people trying to follow the Lord's example have a breaking point. The girl had called me a liar, disrespected my mama, my daddy, and my church. I had been known to fight for less, and I was asking myself why I was trying to be like Jesus when I really just wanted to be like Muhammad Ali.

The very first time Erma and I had met, we had a fight. Without going into too much detail, I'm pretty sure she didn't come to my house now for a repeat of that, 'cause it didn't end in her favor. I was about to let her know where she could go and how she could get there when she told me not to call her when "the man that speaks to God" had us drinking his grape Kool-Aid. Her last words to me were, "You're stupid, and I can't be around stupid people!"

I didn't know what to say or how I should even respond to her. Most of the stuff she said just sounded crazy to me. Nobody was drinking grape nothing up in our church, and if they were, I hadn't been offered any.

The last person I wanted to talk to about the argument that Erma and I had was my mama. My mama is a true Gossip with a capital G, and I am sure she was ear hustling when Erma came by earlier, sounding like she had escaped from the Tower of Babble. My mama kept poking and prodding, trying to get me to tell her what happened without actually asking me what happened. I don't know why Mama was acting like I'm the kid that's gonna go to her seeking advice about how to navigate my way through a friend-fight, because I'm certainly not going to pretend she is the type of mother who will let me vent to her about my friend(s) without her reminding me at some point that I'm the one that told her that my friend was crazy. And, God forbid my friend and I make up and I ask my mother to go someplace with my "crazy" friend. The first thing out of my mama's mouth would be, "Crazy people do crazy things. Crazy is the mother who allows her child to go someplace with a crazy person. Do I look crazy to you?" The last time I told my mama I had a fight with a friend, she was more offended than I was, and to this day that girl isn't welcome in my house.

So I knew that if Erma and I were going to work it out, Mama wasn't the one who was going to talk me through it. Daddy was always more reasonable in these types of situations, but I still knew enough not to tell my dad that the person who sparked the questions was my friend Erma. I found a box of old encyclopedias and pretended like I had read about the Church in it. After I was finished pretending to read and find my own answers, I decided to talk with my father. My dad was pretty levelheaded and could turn some of the most stressful situations into something funny. He explained the history of the Church of Jesus Christ to me as best he could and told me that ultimately I would have to seek the truth for myself and decide how I would respond to people when they confronted me about my decision to join it. Either I believed in what I was doing and where I had chosen to worship or I didn't. He also encouraged me to read about the history of the Church, just as I had to read about United States history.

Daddy helped me understand why Erma said the things she said, but I was still mad at her for the way she exploded on me. I promised myself I'd never speak to her again unless she apologized for accusing me of trying to poison her.

Honestly, I was in shock over the way she reacted to me just because I had decided to join the Church. She had been my bestie every summer since fourth grade. With all the time we spent together, talking about everything under the sun, we had never discussed religion. If I went to visit her, it wasn't unusual for her grandmother to ask me if I'd attended church that day, but other than that we didn't talk about church. It's not like I attended church with her or her grandmother before I joined the Church of Jesus Christ. We weren't even the same religion—they were Baptist, and I was Pentecostal. It just felt so weird to me that she was so angry over nothing. I mean, who argues over religion? She was mad at me for finding a church that I like? If she thought that going off on me, accusing me of being a liar, and claiming that I had put something in her

Kool-Aid that would alter her mental state was going to make me leave my church, she really was crazy!

It was just so random to me, because nothing about our friendship would have made me think she even cared if I went to church or stayed home. She didn't like attending church with her grandmother, and I didn't know if she attended regularly when she was at home. All I could do is follow my dad's advice and learn more about the history of my new church.

At first I was worried, wondering if Erma was ever going to speak to me again. But with all the nasty stuff she said to me, I might be the one not speaking to her. My mama and all my aunts have always said that "people only believe what they want to believe." I am starting to gain a better understanding of their "old lady" sayings. I know who I am, and while I didn't know a lot about the history of the church that I joined, I had been taught to recognize the Spirit, so I was able to recognize when the Holy Ghost testified to me that joining the Church was part of God's plan for me. It does make me feel sad that my friend doesn't agree with my choice, but I usually only see her in the summer anyway.

God's Army,

Tamu

A LATTER-DAY SAINT MADEA

You probably already figured out that we have a Madea* in our lives; we actually have a couple of them, but we want to introduce you to our Latter-day Saint Madea.** Yep, that's right. The Latter-day Saints got a Madea.

Every set of sisters needs a mama, and since God wanted to spare our biomamas the drama, He made us sistas from different mistas and sent us our Madea, our otha motha.

Now, unlike Tyler Perry's Madea, our Madea knows how to read; she knows how to read so well she can read between the lines, so we are going keep her quotes 100 percent. The last thing we want her to accuse us of is lyin' on her. If she's told us once, she has told us a thousand times: "If you lie, you will cheat; if you cheat, you will steal; and if you

> * "Mother Dear"; a term of endearment for an older mother figure; also a fictional character created by Tyler Perry. Madea is the grandma that keeps it real.

> ** Our Madea is err'thang Madea is, plus she is a Latter-day Saint. Which means she will cut you, ask the bishop to give you a blessing, and then make you some Jell-O.

steal, you will kill." And we already know she ain't never coming to visit our behinds in prison.

We have been blessed to have our Madea as a strong woman of faith in our lives. And we're grateful for her many pearls of wisdom. She says, "Sometimes people ain't playin' with a full deck, and you can't reason with crazy." And the bishop better not try to edit her church talks. "This is the talk I wrote. Don't change nothing. If you change it, you give it." She reminds us not to judge by saying, "We don't know their story." And our personal favorite, "We all have the right to hate, but as Christians, when we take upon ourselves the name of Christ, we give up that right."

One of the reasons we lean on her during times of difficulty is that she has the extraordinary gift of being able to experience hard things and stay solid in faith. The scriptures say to "cast thy burden upon the Lord, and he shall sustain thee: he shall never suffer the righteous to be moved" (Psalm 55:22). We've always known that the Lord is willing to share our burden, but our Madea helped us to understand that He will actually bear our burden. She says, "Cast your burden on the Lord . . . and leave that mess with him! Folks always want to give their burdens to the

Lord but then pick them back up again. Naw, when you cast 'em, leave 'em."

People have a tendency to go to others with their problems; they like to call it venting. Some of us don't really understand the concept of a vent, which is an opening that allows air to pass through it. When we air out, it should stay out, but some of us recycle that air. Instead of getting our problems out, we tell them to others and then come back to tell them again and again. And if that's what we are doing to our friends, then you know there is some recycling going on when we talk to the Lord.

Our trepidation in laying and leaving our burdens at the Lord's feet often comes because we can't imagine that anyone actually feels the pain that we do, and if they can't feel the pain, can they really take the problem? Most of us are familiar with the events of Gethsemane, where Jesus bled from every pore. Not only did Christ take our sins upon Him but He also granted us comfort. Have you ever wondered why the Savior needed to suffer so much? He suffered so He could feel our pain and sorrow, too, and it was necessary because how much greater is the comfort of a Comforter that knows *exactly* how you feel?

When our Madea is driving in the car, she loves to listen to gospel music. One of her favorites is "The Battle Is the Lord's." When that song comes on, she always says, "All right, sista girl, you are singing it!" Then she starts singing along, and we can't help but start singing along too. "Be not afraid nor dismayed by reason of this great multitude; for the battle is not yours, but God's" (2 Chronicles 20:15).

Each of us needs to remember that God does not want us to go it alone, and He has promised that He will lift us up in our hour of need. Going green may be good for the earth, but recycling our burdens is not good for the soul. So, cast your burdens on the Lord, and like our Madea says, "Leave 'em there!"

Can I Get an Amen?

Tamu and Zandra

CAN'T NOBODY LOVE ME LIKE JESUS

From Tamu's Diary:

Sunday morning when I left my house, I thought about dropping my kids off at church and catching a matinee at the theater. Thank the Lord and my mama for the spirit of guilt instilled in me. When I was younger I used to complain to my father about feeling guilty for my wrongdoings (before my filter kicked in that said, "Wait, you can't tell grown folks everything!"). Daddy always replied, "Good. You should feel wrong when you are doing wrong." Not that going to a movie on Sunday is wrong, it just isn't something I typically do. We all have an idea of what it means to observe and respect the Sabbath. Like I said, catching a movie isn't typically what I do.

My confession: I have never had a good relationship with Mother's Day. I don't know. It just seems odd to honor someone just for having a baby. I'm sure I'd feel different if it were called Women's Day, and all women got celebrated. It also feels like the "my mom is better than your mom" holiday. To be honest, my best Mother's Day was the year I gave birth to my oldest son. He was born at 12:01 a.m., the first baby born in that hospital that Mother's Day.

This year, instead of making up an excuse for why I needed to leave, I decided to stay for Sunday School, and I'm really happy that I did. Our Sunday School message was *awesome!* The teacher opened the lesson by asking, "What did your mother teach you about prayer?" I'd never really thought about it. As a kid, prayer was like food at my house: it just happened. I don't remember anyone teaching me how to chew food and eat it (actually, I have an aunt that would pinch us for smacking), but I'm pretty sure somebody taught me how to pray.

The more I pondered the question, the more I was able to reflect on the things I learned from my mother and not just about prayer. I also pondered about the spirit and nature of God. My mama was an old skool gospel gangsta. If we didn't make it to church on Sunday, we had church at home, on the television or radio, which usually lasted longer than attending an actual church service.

My mama talked about God and Jesus so much that when I was younger, I thought they were members of my family living somewhere in my house. She made sure we (all of us Thomases, my maiden name) were exposed to God. I knew who God was before I knew what He was. She lived what she believed, and she prayed for what she wanted. Mama had the ability to talk to God like she was talking to her BFF. Because of the relationship she had with God and the Savior, I learned that They were separate, real beings and not ghostly spirits that floated around trying to sneak up on us backsliding.

My mama was also a prayer warrior. She believed it was necessary for everyone who claimed to be in God's army to get up before the enemy did. As a soldier for Jesus, she was usually up at five o'clock putting her daily order in to

God and arming herself with His word. A few times I heard my mama talking to God and thought she was talking to one of my relatives, her conversation was so real. You know what I'm sayin'? When you grow up in a house hearing your mama talk to God the way my mama spoke to Him, not only do you get to know Him but you know that He knows you, too. When my mama prayed for her children, she was direct and specific. If somebody wasn't living right, she prayed about it. If somebody was going through a difficult time at school, at work, or in a relationship, my mama was praying about it. I was a nosey kid, so if any of my mama's friends had asked her to pray for them, I knew their business. But I also knew better than to bring up anything I heard her conversing with the Lord about on behalf of one of her friends.

Knowing that my mama was a prayer warrior was a blessing to me. When I got married and moved out of my parents' home, I knew that no matter what, whether I needed it or not, my husband and I were getting prayed for that day, and at five the next morning my mother was going to be praying for us again. She prayed like she knew He was listening, and she waited, expecting Him to answer her. Because of her positive attitude when it came to making supplications to the Lord, I developed the same type of attitude. I knew that if God wasn't a respecter of persons, and if my mama could talk to Him and expect an answer, I could too. Regardless of my age, because in His eyes, age ain't nothing but a number.

I will never forget the first time I prayed and received an answer. I was at a Little League baseball game with two older cousins. I don't really know why, but my aunt trusted my oldest cousin with the refreshment money. I'm sure she thought he would be fair and buy us treats when we asked him to or told him we were hungry. However, trusting him with the money was the worst decision she could have made. That dude could never be the leader of a country, because it would be a dictatorship. He refused to buy us (his younger brother and me) anything to snack on. Every time we would tell him we were hungry, he would tell us it wasn't time because he wasn't hungry yet. Meaning that we had to wait for him to stop flirting with all the girls and get hungry himself before his brother and I could have something to eat!

Feeling like I might have been better off in an impoverished developing country, I had had enough. I was going to call my aunt! I walked over to the pay phone (with no money, and this was long before the days of mobile devices) and dialed the operator. I told her that I needed to call my aunt because my cousin wasn't sharing, and I was hungry.

While she was very kind, she insisted that I pass the phone to an adult, to which I replied, "I don't know none of these people! I'm at a baseball game, and I'm hungry, lady!" (I wasn't as eloquent back then as I am today.) She told me to stop playing on the phone before the police came and took me to jail. That is all she needed to say to me. To this day I try to avoid dialing the operator.

I stood there at the pay phone, remembering my mother's example, and thought a little prayer couldn't hurt. I didn't get down on my knees or fold my hands. I just stood right there at the phone booth and told God that I was really hungry and that I didn't mind staying at the game if I could eat something, but if my cousin wasn't going to buy me and his brother any food, please send my aunt to get me. Those weren't my exact words, but that's pretty much what I said.

A few minutes later, I was walking past the refreshment stand. I noticed that when one of the men ordering food reached into his pocket to get his money, an extra wad of bills fell out of his pocket, and he was unaware of it. I walked over, picked up the folded bills, and handed them to the man, who was either so shocked at my honesty or so grateful for my honesty (I didn't ask him) that he handed me a wrinkled-up five dollar bill. I did what I'd seen and heard my mama do many times before: I raised my right hand and said out loud, "Thank ya, Jesus!"

At nine years old, I was not only aware of God but aware that God was aware of me. He listened for my voice, and He responded to my voice. I knew what had happened was a blessing, and that single event was just as significant and miraculous to me as manna from heaven was for Moses and the Israelites.

Learning to pray is one thing, but learning to be a prayer warrior was a whole 'nother thing! I don't know if at a certain age faithful people just get a Ph.D. in prayer, but my mama and aunts (all my mama's friends included) got to a place in their relationship with God that they were no longer just faithful Christians praying. I guess they skipped getting their master's, or maybe they were in the master's program by the time I arrived on the scene. Each and every one of them had earned their Ph.D. as far as I was concerned. I'm talking about prayer warriors here. Once they had a cause, it was on like a pot of neck bones!*

I don't know if Nephi, in the Book of Mormon (sound familiar? That's where we members of The

> ✱ Something is about to start, or be "on." Once the water starts boiling in the pot, it's "on."

Church of Jesus Christ of Latter-day Saints got our old nickname "Mormon" from; it's that other book of scripture you'll find next to the Bible in the nightstands at Marriott hotels) would have been able to hang with these women when it came to 2 Nephi 32:9: "But behold, *I say unto you that ye must pray always, and not faint;* that ye must not perform any thing unto the Lord save in the first place ye shall pray unto the Father in the name of Christ, that he will consecrate thy performance unto thee, that thy performance may be for the welfare of thy soul" (emphasis added).

There are some things you might not understand about prayer warriors, especially where my mama was concerned. When it came to the people she loved who stood in need of a blessing, you'd better stay out of her way, 'cause the only thing you could do for her was pray with her. She didn't allow crazy talk! By crazy talk, I mean she didn't lend energy to doubt, not even in playing. Mama used to say, "Where fear exists, faith cannot!" Your faith didn't have to match her faith, but if you opened your mouth and some doubt fell out of it, you had to get out of her face. My mama acknowledged the presence of God, as well as the spirit of Satan, and she didn't mind calling Satan out and then putting him out! She'd announce, "Satan, the Lord rebuke you!" Or, my very favorite, "The devil is a lie!"

Doubt was not welcome in Mama's home. If you didn't have enough faith to stand with her, you'd better take your doubtful behind somewhere else or keep your mouth shut. She taught me that people can either breathe life into you or suck life out of you and the blessings that God intends for you. Let me tell you this right now, my mama didn't mind letting folks know that if they had negative breath, they couldn't come to her house breathing all that negativity on her blessings! According to my mama, negativity is extremely contagious and very dangerous. I developed the same attitude. If folks couldn't breathe on my mama's blessings, I sure didn't need 'em breathing on mine. Shoot, I'm a closet doubter. My testimony might not survive something like that.

Sometimes we don't act like Christians. Sometimes we are actually running around here acting like "tians" (without the *Christ* part). In Ebonics *tians* means "enemy to Jesus." Just kidding. I made that definition up. However, don't you go acting shocked when *tian* ends up in the Urban Dictionary.

Anyway, not long ago a pastor from another church informed me that because I was a Latter-day Saint, I wasn't Christian and that I was no longer part of the black community. I had one of those "pastor puhleeze" moments. His announcement was more amusing than hurtful. Because when I went into the baptismal font I was black, and when I came out of the water, I was still black. The last time I checked, Psalm 51:2 said (urban dictionary translation), "I'm clean. All them sins is gone! Hallelu-yer." That scripture didn't say nothing about all my color, culture, or ethnicity being gone with the sins.

It's a good thing that while my mama was teaching me how to pray, she was also teaching me that even men of God can get it wrong sometimes. That's why we can't trust in the arm of flesh alone. Now that doesn't mean for you to run up on your pastor and say, "Tamu said I can't trust you!" Slow down. I don't want to be the reason you stop going to church. It means that even when your ecclesiastical leaders tell you something, you still need to pray about it.

Don't get me wrong. I know that Latter-day Saints aren't the only Christians getting picked on. Is it just me, or does it seem like some Christians are constantly trying to kick folks out of the Christian Country Club?

After the pastor finished telling me why *he* didn't consider black Latter-day Saints to be Christian and why *he* didn't feel that black Latter-day Saints (me included) were part of the black community, I remembered my mama's teachings. I already told you that she taught me a long time ago that negativity was contagious, so I knew that the man I was talking to didn't have the ability to look at me with his Christian glasses on.

Because of my mama's prayers and the words of affirmation she spoke over me, I've always known who I am and have been comfortable with myself. Being comfortable with myself and having faith in God means that I'm going to reserve my place and actively participate in all my communities. The truth is, just by speaking words, I could stop belonging to almost every cultural group I belong to. But no matter what I say, words won't change my ethnicity. So, to those who claim that black Latter-day Saints are no longer a part of the black community, all I got to say about that is, I'ma pray for you!

My mama's intimate relationship with our Father in Heaven extended beyond prayer. She knew Him, and she knew what He was capable of doing in her life. I'm grateful that she armed me with all the tools I needed to develop a foundational relationship with Him. My mama was ushered into eternity more than ten years ago, but long before she went, she had made sure I had a solid religious foundation, and the religious organization I belong to now helps reiterate the guiding principles she taught me in my youth.

By the time I finished reminiscing in my head about my mama and what she had taught me about prayer, Sunday School was over. But here's what I would have shared with my Sunday School class on Mother's Day: My mama taught me that prayer was personal. She taught me that God could and would communicate with me in my language, so there was no need for me to try to be someone I wasn't. She taught me to believe in my inner voice and to know that I had a direct line of communication with my Father in Heaven. Between my mama, aunts, uncles, and a few cousins, I practically grew up in a theological school. With all the things my mama taught me, it was her example that had the greatest impact.

Daily Doubt Vaccination,

Tamu

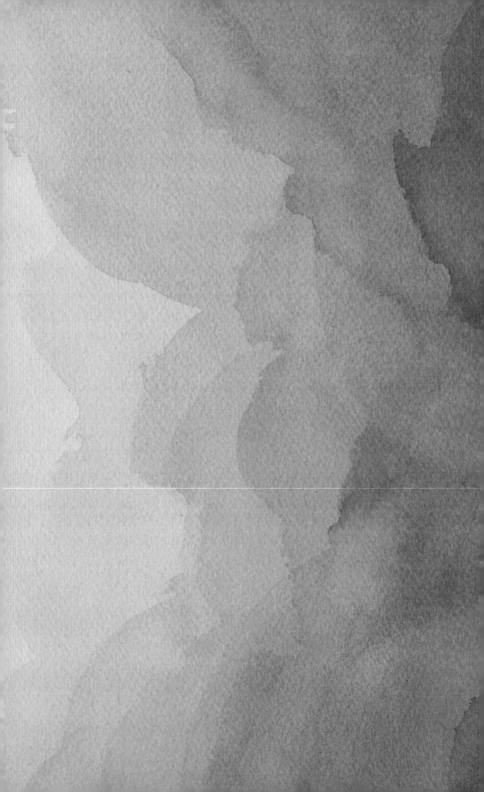

CHAPTER 4

THE NERVE TO SERVE

If you don't serve with love,
then you'll never love to serve.

GO FISH

When it comes to service, nobody should be acting brand-new. It's not a new concept, and we all know we should be doing it. Who doesn't know that if every person lent a hand when they saw a need, the world would be a better place? If you didn't know, now you do. So let's not waste time talking about why we should serve, okay? Let's talk about why we don't serve, and once we cross that bridge, can we puhleez talk about the way we should serve?

The complicated part of service isn't whether it's the right thing to do or if it's the good thing to do. The complicated part of service is people, because people have choices and options. You throw that in the mix, and simple stuff somehow becomes complicated. Now don't get us wrong; options are a good thing. We love options, especially the stock kind.

But options can complicate things too. For instance, you know you need a pair of shoes. That's simple, but when you walk into the mall, according to our husbands, that's when it gets complicated. Now you have a million options of where to buy shoes. And even when you narrow it down to where you want to buy, you gotta pick the style, the color, and, don't forget, the price. Five hours and twenty shopping bags later, your simple shoe-shopping trip is finally complete.

That's the way service works as well. We simply know that we should be serving in our families, communities, and churches, but with all the other life options that demand our time and attention, what we know we should do doesn't always end up being what we actually do. And it's not only time that can complicate service but it's our feelings too.

We know that some men are thinking: No, those are chick problems; women love to complicate everything by bringing emotions into it, but slow your roll,* boys, y'all do it too. Remember that time Michael Jordan and Charles Barkley were doing that "we're BFFs" interview with Oprah? Oprah asked Charles if it was true that Michael Jordan is cheap. You know there are friends

* Hold up; wait a minute.

and then there are Friends. No matter what the truth is, if Friends are on national television, they will opt for the response that is most flattering to their Friend's character.

Well, Michael Jordan and Charles Barkley, they're not that kind of friends. So Charles tells Oprah that one time they were together, and Charles went to give money to a homeless man. Michael slapped Charles's hand and said, "If he can say, 'Do you have any spare change?' then he can say, 'Welcome to McDonald's. Can I help you, please?'" Last time we checked, Michael Jordan was a man. Clearly, these are not just chick problems.

So, yes, we all have emotions about service. We don't want to feel taken advantage of or that we are enabling, and sometimes we may even have bad feelings towards the person, community, or group that we are deciding whether or not to serve.

We need to follow the Savior's example and keep service simple. "Even as the Son of man came not to be ministered unto, but to minister, and to give his life a ransom for many" (Matthew 20:28). Our mission is to minster and to attend to the wants and needs of others. Sometimes we want to give our own version of service: "Give a man a fish, and you'll feed him for a day; teach a man to fish, and you feed him for a lifetime." As we recall, when the multitudes got hungry, Jesus fed five thousand with two fishes and five loaves; he didn't take them on a fishing trip.

Now this is where folks start trippin'.* Teaching is service, so are we just supposed to work hard and enable those who don't work? Again we are to look to Christ's example. Let's go back to the fishes and loaves; do you remember why all those hungry people were even with Jesus in the first place? After John the Baptist was killed, Jesus tried to get some alone time. You know how a mother locks herself in a room for some peace and quiet and the minute the lock clicks, that's when everyone remembers that they need to make some sort of special request that apparently only she can fill? Eventually the whole family is gathered at the closed door being the opposite of quiet, and the only way to get any peace is to open it and find out what they want.

It wasn't exactly like that for Jesus, but thousands of people followed Him and gathered where He was. Even in His time of sadness, Jesus showed compassion and began to bless and teach the people. Jesus was serving through teaching, but He didn't teach them in place of feeding them. There are times when we think we are teaching a

> ✲ Actin' as if there is a problem when there's not; actin' crazy.

man to fish when what we are really doing is holding up our fish and saying, "You know how I got this fish? I went fishing!" And then we walk off smacking our lips 'cause our fish tastes so good.

Withholding is not the same as teaching. So if we walk away, then the next time we see that hungry soul and he's eating some fish, we shouldn't pat ourselves on the back and think, "See how I helped him? Because I refused to give him fish, he went and figured out how to fish." Oh, no. That just means that despite us turning down an opportunity to be God's hand, God found a different way to feed a man.

Can I Get an Amen?

Tamu and Zandra

HOPE FOR THE HOMELESS

From Tamu's Diary:

Sister Plant announced that she had finally heard back from the Food and Care Coalition and that they wanted our Young Women's group to help serve a week from Wednesday. All the other young women were excited, and

I couldn't understand why. You'd think by the way they were acting that they had won the lottery. When I told her that I wouldn't be there, she seemed heartbroken.

"Aww, why not?" she wanted to know. "Are you going to be out of town?"

I told her no.

"You don't have a game, do you?"

"No, I don't have a game," I told her. "I just don't want to go, and it's not really my thang."

She replied, "What do you mean, it's not your thing?"

"I just don't want to go," I told her. "It's not something I'm excited about."

A few days later at Mutual,* instead of having a combined activity,** we went over how our service project would qualify us to pass off certain values in our Young Women Personal Progress books. Sister Plant passed around a list with the names of all the young women and permission slips next to a check-off box so that each young woman could indicate which values she wanted to work on. After

* Weekday meeting of youth groups in the Church of Jesus Christ.

** Weekday activity for both boys' and girls' youth groups.

class, Sister Plant asked me if I had given our service project any more thought.

"Not really," I said.

Sister Plant drove us home, and when the other girls were out of the car, Sister Plant started trying to Jedi mind-trick me. She talked about how the last time they had served it was such a wonderful bonding experience and how they all felt spiritually edified, because they knew they were doing the Lord's work. I didn't need a service project at a homeless shelter to serve others. If what she says is true, I've been doing the Lord's work most of my life, because I have a whole lot of folks that I serve on a regular basis. Being the oldest of eight kids and living with or near all my younger cousins, I was constantly serving someone. I could have told Sister Plant a thing or two about service, what it required, and how I felt about it. I didn't receive a personal witness, and the people I served hardly ever said thank you. So she wanted me to leave my regular unpaid service position to go serve a whole bunch of people that I didn't know or care to know. Sister Plant had it twisted. She didn't know me as well as she thought she did.

When she pulled up to my house, she parked her car, which I thought was odd considering she usually just dropped me off.

"Thanks for the ride, Sister Plant," I said as I opened my door.

Sister Plant said, "No problem," as she was taking off her seat belt.

"What are you doing? Do you have to use the bathroom?" I asked.

Sister Plant looked at me and smiled. "No, I just need to speak with Sister Thomas about a situation that I'm dealing with. I'd really like to get her opinion on it."

Sometimes teenagers aren't very bright, or maybe it was just me. Sister Plant took a seat in our living room and I went to find my mama. I thanked Sister Plant again for the ride and went about my business.

The next Sunday in Young Women, Sister Plant was acting unusually happy. She announced again that we would be visiting the homeless shelter and that we'd be working toward completing some of the Young Women values. She again passed around the list of values that we'd be working on. This time when I looked at the list there was a check by my name.

"Umm, Sister Plant, I believe someone made a mistake. I didn't turn in a permission slip."

She had a twinkle in her eye. "I know. When I was speaking to your mother the other day, I told her about the service project, and she thought it would be a great idea if you attended, so I ran out to the car and got her a permission slip to sign. She filled everything out before I left."

Pretending to be shocked, she said, "She didn't talk to you about it?" Sister Plant knew very well my mama hadn't talked to me about going to the homeless shelter.

I know I was looking like "Uh Duh." I had gotten bamboozled by an older (she was maybe thirty at the time) white lady. I trusted her when she said that she needed to talk to my mother about a situation. I just didn't know that *I* was the situation Sister Plant had to discuss with my mama.

I sat through Young Women silent and upset, trying to figure out how I was going to explain to my mama why I didn't want to go. On the way home with my friend and her parents, my friend kept going on and on about how excited she was to go to the homeless shelter. The more I tried to stay calm, the angrier I got.

"Do you realize we are going to be working with the crazy people, the lazy people, and the addicts that can't hold it together? Some of these people are probably even killers hiding out from the police at the homeless shelter," I said. I had snapped! I realized that watching *America's Most Wanted* wasn't good for me.

Everyone in the car got quiet. Brother Bannum, my friend's father, kept looking at me through the rearview mirror. He finally spoke, letting me know that most of what I assumed homeless people to be was not only inaccurate but untrue. He told me that we are not here to judge; we are here to serve. Before I got out of the car, Brother Bannum, paraphrasing scripture, said, "If you've done it unto the least of these, you've done it unto the Savior" (see Matthew 25:40).

Everybody was so gung-ho about service and not judging people, yet I felt like they were judging me because they thought I was judging others. Mama was in the front room speaking to my aunt on the phone when I walked in and slammed the door. I heard my mama say, "Netti, I'm going to have to call you back, 'cause this girl has lost her li'l mind."

Before I could slam my bedroom door, Mama was standing right behind me. "Slam another door if you want to, and see what happens. Are you crazy?"

Is it just me, or does everyone's parents seem to tower over them like giants when they are angry? My mama towered over me with her hands on her hips and all. "What's wrong with you?"

"I told Sister Plant that I didn't want to do that service project. Then she went behind my back, and you told her I would. I'm not going." The minute I said it, I regretted it. I knew Mama was going to take it as a personal challenge.

"Why don't you want to go?"

Mama still had her hands on her hips, but her expression was a lot softer. I had just told her that I wasn't going to do something, and she asked me why I didn't want to. This was a new experience for me, and to tell you the truth, I didn't know how to respond, but she was waiting for me to.

"I don't want to go because I don't want the other young women or the leaders to associate me with the homeless people."

I could tell my mama was confused. "Why would they associate you with the homeless people?"

I knew I had to make my argument without getting too emotional. Crying was not tolerated during explanations unless you'd been in a fight and gotten beat up. She had given me a platform to express my opinion, and the least I could do was trust her with the truth.

"Mama, I don't want to be associated with the homeless people. Every time I go somewhere with white members of the Church, if I say hi or smile at anybody black, they ask me how I know that person. If the homeless people are black, and they probably will be, they are going to ask me if I know them."

I could tell Mama was holding in a laugh, and it was making me want to go into greater depth with my explanation.

"I don't want members of the Church to associate me with the homeless people, and I don't want the homeless people to think they have anything in common with me except the color of our skin."

Still holding back her laughter, Mama looked at me like I was a stranger in her house. She told me to get a life! That was an indication I had tap danced on her last good nerve. The softness that I had recognized earlier was gone. There was no honey in her voice, no laughter in her eyes. She said, "You are going to that shelter! You are going to be kind to the people there! Especially the black people! You will serve all of your brothers and sisters, and you will do it with a happy heart! So whatever you got to do to make that happen, you'd better do it! Step outside yourself, and check your attitude!" When she turned to walk away, she was still talking. "I don't know who she thinks she is, talkin' 'bout she don't want to be associated with the black people if they're homeless. I don't know where this li'l girl came from, but I know she is going to that homeless shelter."

I felt conflicted and embarrassed. I probably would have been better off telling Sister Plant why I didn't want to go. I'm sure she would have been more sympathetic toward my situation than my mama was. From then on until the service project, I did my best to avoid my mama. Whenever she looked at me, it was that "um um um, you po' pitiful child!" That's not what she said; that's how her look made me feel. By the time the service project rolled around, I had started to feel a bit of excitement myself. Not because I was excited to go to the homeless shelter like the other young women, but because I was ready for the whole ordeal to be over with.

Sister Plant came to pick me up, and right before I walked out of the door, my mama handed me an envelope. She told me to give it to Sister Plant because she'd know what to do with it.

Then Mama reminded me that since I had to serve anyway, I might as well serve with a happy heart.

"You don't know how difficult it is for some people to have to accept help. You need to smile at them and be gracious to them because at this point all they got is a little bit of hope and dignity. So you need to get over your hang-ups and have a happy heart! 'Cause if you have a happy heart, your face will follow." She told me that she was proud of me and that she loved me.

I walked out to Sister Plant's car thinking about what my mama had said about homeless people having only a little hope and dignity. I tried to have a happy heart, and I tried to get over myself, but the closer we got to the homeless shelter, the faster my heart beat. I don't know who or what I was afraid of, but I was afraid.

I knew nothing bad was going to happen, but the fear of not knowing what to expect was creating even more anxiety for me. We were all given jobs and shown the correct serving portions. My job was to scoop up potatoes and place them on the trays. Easy enough, I thought. After we were finished serving the homeless, we were supposed to serve each other and eat in the dining room with the homeless people. The thought of breaking bread with homeless people was enough to send my nervous system into shock. That was something that was left out of the entire conversation when Sister Plant spoke to us.

I looked at Sister Plant, who was standing right next to me, and asked, "Are we eating with them?"

After hearing her nervous laugh, I didn't need to hear anything else, but she said, "I thought you knew that.

That's one of the reasons we love serving here. We get to interact with the brothers and sisters that we serve. It makes them feel good to know that we aren't just here to give to them but that we want to get to know them, too."

I wasn't really focused on what Sister Plant said after she said we were eating together. I started silently chanting, "Have a happy heart, and your face will follow."

We were almost finished serving when I thought I saw a familiar face approaching. I had just gotten my heart to calm down, and now it was beating so hard, it was about to burst through my shirt. I was sure that everyone standing near me could see my chest moving. I thought about making a mad dash to the bathroom to avoid him but it was too late. Joe, a kid from school, was standing right in front of me, even though I had already given him a scoop of mashed potatoes. Our eyes met, but neither of us said anything. What was he doing here? Maybe there was another youth group. Maybe he had been doing a service project with his group in another part of the shelter. I tried not to stare at him, but as soon as he turned to walk toward his table, I couldn't help but stare. He wasn't with a youth group; he was with his family, his mother, sisters, and a brother.

After Joe and his family came through the service line, there were only a few more people who needed dinner.

Then we started filling dinner trays for each other so that we could join our less fortunate brothers and sisters. Sister Plant had invited me to join her at the table where she was sitting. I'm sure she wanted to keep an eye on me and make sure I had an opportunity to mix and mingle and not run and hide in the bathroom until dinner was over like I wanted to. I grabbed my tray of food and headed out to the dining area to look for Sister Plant.

Why, Lord? Why was Sister Plant sitting at Joe's table? I thought about turning around and looking for another leader to sit with, but not only had Joe already seen me see him but Sister Plant called my name.

"Have a happy heart, and your face will follow!" I said to myself. I hope my outside didn't look like what I felt on the inside. I sat at the table almost directly across from Joe. Joe had obviously gotten over our initial sighting of one another.

"What's up? What are you doing here?" Joe was looking directly at me. I don't know if he was trying to read me or if he was just that cool.

It took me a minute as I kept thinking about what my mama had told me.

"Nothing. What's up with you?"

Sister Plant asked, "Do you guys know each other?"

I looked at Joe and waited for him to answer because I didn't know what to say. The truth was yes, we knew each other, but I didn't want to tell people because sometimes Latter-day Saints, and I'm sure other Christian groups have similar experiences, can be so nosey. I knew that as soon as we got into the car, Sister Plant was going to be all up in Joe's business, asking me all types of questions.

Sister Plant asked again, "Do you two know each other?" She called me by name and asked me that question a third time. I still wasn't saying anything!

Joe must've realized I wasn't going to say anything, so he answered Sister Plant. "Yeah, we go to school together. We even have a few classes together."

Sister Plant seemed pleased that someone had finally answered her and didn't risk asking either of us another question. Instead she focused her attention on Joe's mother.

Joe said, "You didn't answer my question. What are you doing here? Is that your mom?"

I looked at Sister Plant and then back at Joe. "Are you blind?"

At which Joe started laughing at how absurd his question was.

Let me give y'all a visual. Sister Plant and I are at opposite ends of the color spectrum. There is no way in the world that Joe thought I was Sister Plant's daughter. Now, before we start getting letters from white mothers with black children or black children with white mothers, I was a teenager then and had not yet been exposed to families that adopted transracially.

Joe's question helped to break the ice. I told him I was with a young women's group from my church and that we came to the shelter to serve, eat, and mingle with our brothers and sisters here. Joe thought that was cool. He told me that his parents had gotten a divorce and that his mother had lost her job a while ago. Unable to pay the house note, his family slept in their car at night and ate and showered at the shelter. His mom couldn't stay in the shelter because he and his brother were too old to sleep there, and his mother didn't want him and his brother sleeping in the car alone in the neighborhood.

Listening to Joe share his story, I felt sad and guilty. I had categorized homeless people, creating reasons for why their life's situation was what it was. It had never occurred to me that children were homeless, but it makes sense that if adults are homeless, then the children they are responsible for will be homeless too. I never imagined that someone I went to school with could be homeless and I not know it. I thought about all the harsh things I'd said and the reasons I'd given for not wanting to go serve at the homeless shelter, and they seemed so trivial to me. What if Jesus had decided He didn't want to go visit the lepers because people might assume He had leprosy?

As I listened to Joe and thought about his family and their situation, I felt sad. Not so much for him as for myself. Even though he wasn't in the best position, he seemed content. He possessed joy that most of the kids at our school seemed to lack. Fear had almost robbed me of an experience that made me feel closer to God. I had been close to passing up an opportunity to serve someone I thought highly of and respected because that opportunity hadn't seemed to fit me. I wondered how many opportunities like this I'd passed up in the past. I was so worked up about having to go to the homeless shelter that I forgot that I actually enjoy serving others. Serving others gives me purpose; it makes me feel like God is working through me to help fulfill the needs of those who can't do it for themselves.

As soon as I walked into the house, my mama, who quoted the Bible for everything, said, "'And the King shall answer and say unto them, Verily I say unto you, inasmuch as ye have done it unto one of the least of these my brethren, ye have done it unto me.' Girl, how does it make you feel to know you were serving the Lord today?"

That scripture from Matthew 25:40 and her comment were sort of like insurance for my mama; it was her preemptive strike. If I had had a bad experience, I couldn't tell her now, especially knowing that if I had done it unto the least, I had done it unto Him. I was grateful. Grateful for a mother who saw the importance of making me step outside myself and serve, and even more grateful for a mother who wasn't afraid to let her children see her serving those in need.

As our talk ended, she reminded me, "Blessings come to those who serve!"

Yes, they do!

Sincerely Your Servant,

Tamu

PEOPLE AREN'T PROJECTS

When we consider all that God has done in our lives, how often do we consider if we are doing what He expects us to do in the lives of others? Taking on the name of Christ means that we are actively seeking opportunities to serve others on behalf of our Father in Heaven. Becoming a Christian means that not only are we servants to Him but also, because He spent His life in nondiscriminatory service to us, we are obligated to serve each other.

Service is not only about providing for the material needs of others during times of emergency or holiday seasons. A lot of us feel compassionate during Thanksgiving, but the reality is people still need food in July, and we don't have to wait until a hurricane hits before we donate to the Red Cross. In fact, the service that is most often needed and the one we are most reluctant to give is our time.

You know what term we understand but we sometimes can't stand? Service Project. A project is an undertaking with an expiration date, and if service is love, then how can it expire? Participating in service projects is wonderful, but we need to remember that the project is the thing we are doing, such as collecting clothes or filling bowls at the soup kitchen. Love is the reason for the service. People are not projects.

Can I Get an Amen?

Tamu and Zandra

SERVICE MAKES ME NERVOUS

From Zandra's Diary:

I do not come from money. I come from whatever the opposite of money is. My siblings and I joke with our parents that we are in a first world country living a third world life. Coming from humble means has made me a lot of who I am today, and it makes me grateful for even the smallest of things. But when I was younger, I didn't have such an appreciation for my family's meagerness. We were blessed because a lot of people served us and showed kindness, but there are experiences I have had that make it hard for me to accept service. I had a love-hate relationship with the Christmas season when I was younger. I loved focusing on the birth of the Savior, seeing the lights and all the festivity, but Christmastime was always a reminder of how poor I was and of what would not be under my family's tree.

One year was especially thin; I was around ten or eleven, I think. We couldn't even afford to get a Christmas tree that year. It was Christmas Eve, and we heard a knock on the door. When we opened the door, there was a tree on the front steps with presents and food all around it. I can still remember all the chatter. We just couldn't believe it. My siblings and I were debating who this could have come from because there was no note. Some were sure it was Santa; some thought it was kind strangers. All were happy and filled with delight. We pulled everything into the house and my parents had us offer a prayer. It took forever for my parents to get us to bed that night. I just remember lying in my bed with a big ole grin on my face.

At that point, it was one of the few times in my life I had ever looked forward to waking up Christmas morning. Years of disappointment had tainted the Christmas morning buzz for me. I had long ago decided that Santa didn't care about little black kids who lived on Johnson Ferry Road. And the last time I had sat on Santa's lap a few years earlier, I made sure to let him know my sentiments. It must have made him mad because he and his elves brought us even less that year. After that, I figured I had better bow out of the visiting Santa thing because I didn't want my mouth to cost everybody gifts.

That Christmas morning we said another family prayer and ate breakfast, and then finally my parents unleashed us, and we let wrapping paper fly. I don't remember all the things I got that year, but I do remember we got a lot. One of the things I remember getting was a beautiful watch. The following Sunday I was so excited to wear it to church. When my friends and I were sitting around chatting in

Primary, people showed off a few items they were wearing that they had gotten for Christmas. I pointed out my new watch, and we all ooed and awed over each other's presents.

Then one of the girls said to me, "Actually, you're wearing my watch."

"No, I'm not," I said.

"Yes, you are," she said. "On Christmas Eve, my parents let us open one gift, and the gift was a surprise family trip to Australia that we were leaving on that night. Then my parents asked what we wanted to do with all our Christmas presents and our tree since we wouldn't be home for Christmas. We took a vote on if we wanted to let poor people have our tree and presents. Everyone else voted yes, but I voted no," she said. "I wanted to open our gifts when we got back from the trip. Well, I was outvoted, so we had to give everything to your family."

I felt as if smoke was coming out my ears. "Well, you can have your watch back," I said, "and all the other presents, too, 'cause I don't want them."

"No. Mom will get mad at me," she told me flippantly.

The other girls were looking around, unsure of what to do or say. I was so humiliated! I was the poor person she had given her Christmas to—under duress. I didn't say a word for the next two hours.

When church was over, I marched through the halls looking for one of my parents. I found my mother first. "Who gave us the stuff on the porch?" I said angrily.

"Santa," she said.

"Really?" I said. "Because unless Santa's real name is Brother Woolard, then I don't think so." I could tell from the look on my mother's face that she knew exactly who had donated Christmas to us, and she was shocked that I knew.

"Who told you that?" she asked.

"It doesn't matter," I replied. "I'm never wearing this watch again, and I don't want any of those other presents, either."

My mother stood there confused as I stormed off to the car.

Later that night she asked me if I was ready to tell her what had happened. When I explained my humiliating ordeal, she tried to comfort me by saying it didn't matter who gave us the gifts. What mattered is that God helped someone to see that we were in need. She implored me to see it as a blessing.

It didn't change how I felt, though. It was just one more reason why I knew I shouldn't accept help from others. My young mind could only put together that people help you because they look down on you. After that, whenever a box of clothes showed up at the house and my mother tried to give me something, I would play Twenty Questions. Where did it come from? Whose is it? Why don't they want it anymore? How do they know us? On and on and on. If I got the wrong answer to just one question, then I didn't want whatever it was.

It's a hard habit to break. Even as an adult I am skeptical of help. When I do have an experience of someone helping me without burning me or wanting anything in return, it sometimes still shocks me. But those shocks help to break down my walls just a little.

Yes, service makes me nervous, but it is okay to let others serve me. When I ask God for food, I would much rather it start raining manna from heaven, but that's not how He seems to be answering prayers these days. Heavenly Father uses us to answer the prayers of our sisters and brothers. When a kind neighbor brings by a meal, that is the Lord answering my prayer. So I must humble myself, let go of my pride, and show gratitude because when I called God and God called them, they answered the call.

Called to Be Served,

Zandra

THE NERVE TO SERVE

WHY YOU ASKING ALL THEM QUESTIONS?

Service can make a lot of us nervous. There are even a few prophets in the scriptures who seem to have felt this way. When most people think of Moses, they remember he's the one who parted the Red Sea so the Israelites could escape Pharaoh. Yeah, that happened, but that's only part of the story. Not only did Moses give us the Ten Commandments but he also gave us a lot of excuses for why he didn't think he could do what the Lord needed him to do.

As the story goes, God appeared to Moses through a burning bush and told him something had to be done to get the Israelites out of bondage. Moses agreed, right up until the point God let him know the somebody was him. (Ain't that a trip, you praying and asking God for an answer, and God makes you the answer to your own prayer?) That's when the excuses started. "Who am I?" Moses asked (Exodus 3:11).

We can certainly understand Moses's dilemma. He was probably thinking, Who am I that Pharaoh would release the Israelites to me? God, you know I killed somebody! I'm on the run. I can't go back to Egypt—I'm a wanted man!

God's response was quick and simple, and for all intents and purposes, it should have ended the conversation. He told Moses, "I will be with you."

To which Moses responded, "What shall I say?" That's excuse number two. Are you for real, Moses? Why you askin' all them questions? God, being the patient parent, simply says, "Tell them, I Am that I Am."

Moses had yet another excuse. "They won't believe me or listen to what I have to say." Black mamas in Egypt are just like black mamas everywhere else: they got black-mama sayings. Moses's mama probably had already told him, "God ain't gonna have your back without having your front, too!" But he was determined to make God say it.

Doesn't it seem like Moses is doing a whole lot of doubting? Moses must have worn God out, 'cause after this interaction, the next person who doubted Him got put on mute. Zacharias probably didn't realize that Moses might have had a li'l something to do with his getting struck dumb.

The most nerve-wracking service can be when God has made the call. In fact, if our caller ID could show us when God was calling, how many of us would be like Moses and hesitate to pick it up? God is not a bill collector; we don't have to be afraid to answer His call. "Look unto me in every thought; doubt not, fear not" (Doctrine and Covenants 6:36).

We should all embark on service with hearts full of peace. God never asks us for anything without providing a way.

Can I Get an Amen?

Tamu and Zandra

PAY IT FORWARD

From Tamu's Diary:

As a child growing up in the city, I often saw people panhandling on the off-ramps of freeways, in front of stores, or, most often, on street corners. One day after hearing my parents talking about their lack of money and being unable to afford all the needs of their needy children, I ventured out with my mama to the market to buy some groceries. As we were leaving the store, we were approached by a young woman who looked a hot mess. I didn't hear what she said to my mother, but I remember my mother reaching into her bosom and surrendering our family's livelihood, at least our family's livelihood until my father's next payday.

In protest, I reminded my mama about her earlier conversation with my dad in hopes she wouldn't forget that the money she had just withdrawn from her bra bank was all we had.

Before I could finish, my mama stopped me. In front of the young woman, she told me that she was well aware of what my father had said, and unless I was paying the bills at 1283, I should stay out of grown folks' business and mind my own before she gave me some to mind. (These are the kinds of threats black Latter-day Saint mamas give their kids. They make no sense but will make you straighten up and fly right in a hurry.)

In the car, my mama looked at me and said, "Paid it forward." I wanted to give her side-eye stink-eye for embarrassing me in front of that grungy-looking girl but opted out for several reasons. Mostly because she was the type of mama that didn't mind putting a kid out of the car.

"Paid it forward?" I repeated.

Without taking her eyes off the road, my mama said, "Yes. That girl hasn't always looked like that. She is someone's daughter, someone's princess; she is hungry, cold, tired; and she misses her family. I gave her what I could to help her because I would want someone to do the same for you or one of your sisters if I'm not there to help you. I felt inspired to help her, so I did. If your daddy is mad, he can be mad at the Spirit, 'cause I paid it forward!"

My Mama's Princess,

Tamu

DO NOT PASS HIM BY

As Christians, we declare that we don't live our lives for nobody but Jesus. Well, that's what we say, but is that what we do? Anyone who has accepted Jesus as their personal Savior would jump at the chance—shoot, fight for the chance—to give back to Christ in honor of the gift that He has given us. Yet every day we pass Jesus by. Christ tells us that the righteous are those who care for the hungry, the thirsty, the strangers, the naked, the sick, and the imprisoned. What we need to ask ourselves is who were we hanging with yesterday and who are we about to go see today? Anyone on the aforementioned list?

Some of us don't have a problem serving God as long as we get to pick what and how we get to serve. If we truly have a desire to serve God, then we must look at those who give us opportunities to serve as the blessings they really are. When Jesus was crucified, as He hung on the cross near death, He spoke the words "I thirst" (John 19:28). Not one of us would deny our Lord and Savior, so we must remember that the only way we have to quench Jesus's thirst is to offer one of our brothers or sisters on this earth a beverage, for He says, "Inasmuch as ye have done it unto one of the least of these my brethren, ye have done it unto me" (Matthew 25:40).

Can I Get an Amen?

Tamu and Zandra

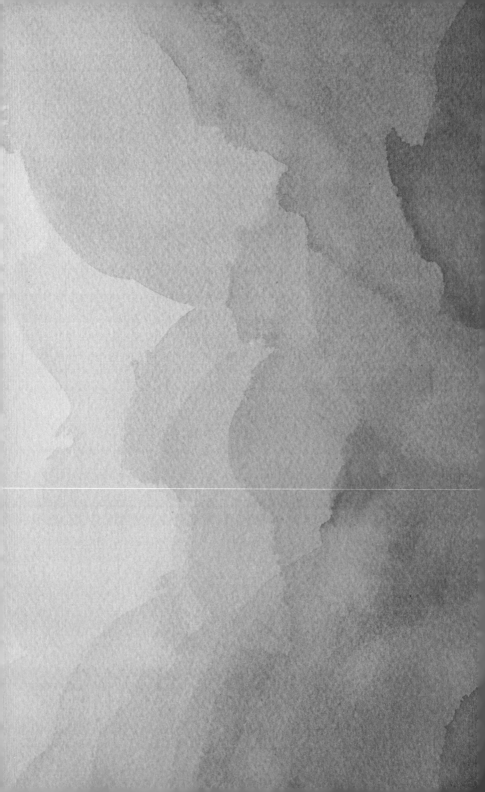

CHAPTER 5

BEGGING FOR CHANGE

> Excuse me, can you spare any change?
> Not from the pocket but of the heart.

SPARE CHANGE

"Excuse me. Can you spare any change?" We've all heard those words as we've hurried along the sidewalk or walked through a doorway. The voice of a beggar always causes a response. Some of us keep moving and pretend we didn't hear. Others of us immediately reach into our pockets in search of what we have to give to the hand in need. And there are those of us who have programmed our automated response system to automatically respond with a polite, "I'm sorry. I don't have any cash on me." In short, no.

The funny thing about spare change is that it really is often unwanted. We check out of the store, and when the cashier goes to give us our pennies, we reply, "Keep the change." Spare change in the form of coins is heavy; it weighs our pockets down. We would much rather have thin, neat bills, which can be folded and slid into our wallets. Bills are so much easier to carry than change.

Yes, loose change can be burdensome, yet when the beggar asks for it, it is sometimes not given freely. The term *beggar* is so full of negative connotations. Some of us have parents like the ones who snatch you up before you go into an event and say, "Don't go up in there beggin' for food like I didn't just feed you at home." Nobody wants to be called a beggar or be accused of begging.

In the book of Mosiah, in the Book of Mormon, King Benjamin gathered all the people together to school them on a few things. He talked to them about Jesus, repentance, and forgiveness. He basically gave them a mega-church sermon long before TD Jakes, Joel Osteen, Creflo Dollar, or Oprah and her Life Class were even a twinkle in their daddy's eye. During his sermon King Benjamin dropped this bit of knowledge: "For behold, are we not all beggars? Do we not all depend upon the same Being, even God, for all the substance which we have, for both food and raiment, and for gold, and for silver, and for all the riches which we have of every kind?" (Mosiah 4:19).

You know somebody somewhere was sitting there listening to King Benjamin and saying, "I know he's not talking to me. I have never begged for anything from anybody a day in my life!" And if way back, back, back in the day was anything like back in our day, then somebody replied, "I beg your pardon? I might be mistaken, but it sho looked like you were doing a whole lot of beggin' when you asked homegirl to go out with you and she had to tell you no several times." Whether we want to admit it or not, the reality is that we are all beggars, and like the panhandler, we too are begging for change.

Just as with spare change, we often find making change in our lives to be a heavy and cumbersome burden; we do not give it so freely. When our lives are begging for change, we may respond with the same options we give the person on the street corner. Some of us dig deep and immediately search for changes within ourselves. Others ignore the need for changes, and yes, some of us respond with, "I'm sorry. I can't spare the time for change right now." In short, no.

Unlike with money, our spiritual finances always have the budget to allow us to make some change. So why, when we can afford it, do we deny ourselves, the beggar, the change?

Can I Get an Amen?

Tamu and Zandra

PENNIES FROM HEAVEN

When you begin stages of self-improvement, it can get rough, because these new behaviors are usually the opposite of what you've been inclined to do. Good doesn't mean easy, so just because we have the desire to form good habits doesn't mean we'll be able to do so effortlessly. But we can't let that deter us. If you call out to God and say, "Lord, a dollar sure would change my life right now," and immediately four quarters drop from the sky and fall on your head, you can't look up and yell, "Ouch! You could have dropped a dollar bill!" If you do that, and He says, "I didn't have any ones on me; all I had were coins," are you going to reply, "Well, those quarters hit me hard, so next time I ask for a blessing, don't give it to me if all you have on you is change"? Don't tie God's hands. Allow Him to do what He wants, when He wants, and how He wants to do it.

Making worthwhile changes in our lives is often our signal to Heavenly Father that we are willing to accept the blessings that He has been longing to bestow upon us. Desire to change doesn't automatically equal success, but faith plus willingness will light the way. If we lean on the Lord during the process of changing, He will give us strength where we are weak, patience when we are at our wits' end, and confirmation that though positive change may not be easy, it is always worth it.

Can I Get an Amen?

Tamu and Zandra

SWEARING TO CHANGE

From Zandra's Diary:

I've decided I'm gonna stop cussing. Now, I'm not talking about Latter-day Saint cussing. Some of you may not even know there is such a thing as Latter-day Saint swear words; they're what some folks call clean curse words. Instead of saying the actual swear word, they use an alternative. Latter-day Saints seem to be particularly fond of certain alternatives, such as oh my heck, gosh dang it, or fetch. Yeah, I'm not talking about those. I'm talking swearing like a sailor.

In case my mama reads this, let me go on record as saying, this hot mouth of mine is not something I picked up at home. And clean cussing—my mum don't play that! One time my sister got popped in the mouth at the grocery store for saying the F word. I didn't hear the exchange, just the pop. Every kid knows the sound of their own mama's smack, and by the time I found them in the cereal aisle, I don't think my dazed sister knew the difference between a cornflake and a Coco Puff. I knew Mum was hot by the way she was talking. See, I have an island mama, and when she gets mad, she starts speaking in tongues, and by tongues I mean English. It's a special kind of English they teach at island mama school. The general translation is yeah, she mad. She real mad.

"Lawd, Fadda, Jesus, give me strength! But I nevah see more, mah own chile have de nerve to cuss me in de grocery store! I doh know who she tink she is, but ah go find out!" Now I was really scared, 'cause the only thing worse than your mad mama talking to you, is your mad mama talking to Jesus . . . about you . . . out loud . . . in public.

"You cussed at Mum?" I asked my sister.

My sister started to speak but not quick enough, 'cause Mum answered for her. "Yes! De F word."

My sister tried to speak again, but my mother was through with all the words in all the world. "Yah see you? I doh' want tah hear not even one peep out you, and if yah even so much as open yah mouth again, you go find out."

Look, anybody who knows my mother knows that what you want to do is the opposite of "find out." 'Cause

I have "found out" before, and it wasn't pretty. My sister shut her mouth tight enough to look obedient but not so tight that it looked like she had an attitude. I shut my mouth too, 'cause I already knew that Captain Crunch, Tony the Tiger, and the Lucky Charm leprechaun combined wouldn't be able to save my sister or me when my mother snapped from the cereal aisle to the candy aisle and had us tasting the rainbow.

All the way home, my mother talked to Jesus about my sister, and I'm not sure what Jesus was saying back to her, but it wasn't all that helpful, because when we got home, my mother flung the door open and yelled my father's name like the house was on fire. My sister was probably wishing that the house was actually on fire, and while Mum told Daddy about her grocery store F-capade, all of us kids were looking for exits so we could evacuate the building.

My sister, in a last-ditch effort to save her life, blurted out, "I didn't say the F word."

"What did you say?" I asked.

My sister was too smart to say it again, so she said she would write it. My parents stood there, so she took a chance, grabbed some scrap paper and a pencil, and scribbled something. My mother refused to look at it so I picked it up and read it.

"Well?" said my father.

"Mum doesn't like the word I said, but it's not *the* F word."

"Oh yes it is," said my mother.

My father took the paper and read it, and then he showed it to my mother. "Yes, that is exactly what she said," said my mother.

"That's not the F word," said my father.

"Well, what's the F word?" my mother said, looking puzzled.

My father leaned over and whispered something into her ear.

Her eyes got big, and she said, "Well, they're both F words."

My father tried to explain to her that one was a substitute for the other, but she didn't care. I'm not even going to tell you what my sister actually said, 'cause I don't need my mama having a flashback and flashing on me if she reads this, but it wasn't *the* F word and that is *the* only thing that saved my sister's life that day. So what everybody in my mama's house needs to know is, there are no clean curse words.

Remember when I said that when my mother says "you'll find out" that you don't really want to find out? This is how I know that. I said my first swear word in seventh grade. Our teacher had left the classroom, I'm minding my business, and this chick starts telling me how I need a perm 'cause my hair is nappy. So I tell her that instead of worrying about my happy-nappy behind, what she should be focusing on is that tired tacky ponytail extension on top of her head. She might be laughing now 'cause I got some kinks in my kitchen, but she wouldn't be laughing anymore once I came over there and pulled that mess off of her. Of course, that is precisely when the teacher walked back into the classroom. Long story short, I got suspended for three days, which was nothing compared to the punishment my folks doled out at home. After that I was too scared to swear for over a decade!

Then as a grown woman with grown people's trials and tribulations, Pandora's box was reopened and, well, I found colorful language a hard habit to break. In my life, I have faced what I would consider some very cuss-worthy trials, and a few years ago when I was enduring several of those tribulations, I happened to be on an airplane. Now know this, except for the time in seventh grade and the experience I'm about to share, my swearing has been to myself or in front of close friends or family (oh, the perks of being in my inner circle). I'm not in the habit of cussing people out, but if you were on this flight, you sure wouldn't know that.

A flight attendant thought I had an electronic device turned on. I didn't, but she kept coming to my seat to ask me to turn the already-switched-off item off. After having my device checked several times and hearing plenty of snide comments, I'd had enough. I went off. Now when I say off, I mean OFF. I think I called this woman everything but a child of God. She was snapping, I was snapping, and she eventually told me she would have the police waiting for me when I got off the flight.

This all happened within the first ten minutes of a three-hour flight, so I went to sleep. She went about her business, and we didn't say a word to each other for the next two hours and fifty minutes. After the plane landed, as I made my way to the exit, a woman put her hand on my shoulder and stopped me.

She said, "Excuse me, are you Mormon?"

My mouth fell open. I started hyperventilating and wishing I had paid attention when the flight attendant was telling us how to apply the oxygen mask and open the emergency exits. As my very loud swear-filled exchange with the flight attendant replayed in my mind, I said,

"Actually, I'm Catholic." Just kidding, I didn't say that. Don't worry, my Catholic brothas and sistas, I wouldn't make another religion claim my bad behavior.

To my utmost despair, I replied, "Yes." Then I just stood there, waiting for her to tell me how I was the worst Latter-day Saint she had ever met or how she was taking the missionary discussions and now because of my cuss-fest she was going to stop. Instead, she pointed to her husband and said, "We are too."

As my very un-Christlike conduct flashed before my eyes again, I thought, "Jesus, take the wheel!" I'm serious. I really was frantically praying in my head. In that moment, I felt so ashamed of myself, but thankfully our God is an *awesome* God, and He answered His desperate child's plea for help.

Now this is the part where God testifies to me that He is real. They didn't even hear my profanity-laced tongue-lashing. I kept waiting for them to say something about it, and they never did; they just kept making pleasant conversation. We said "Nice to meet you" and "Good-bye" and headed off in our separate directions.

Then I hear, "M'am, can we talk to you?" At this point not only had Jesus taken the wheel but He was also doing all the talking. I had a pleasant conversation with the officers, after which they apologized for my unpleasant flight experience . . . po-po, say what?!?

Immediately, I decided I wanted to clean up my language, because clearly, private habits could become public habits, and I never wanted to be in a situation again where my conduct made me ashamed to say that I am a Christian. So that's how I ended up on this journey of how to be a cuss-free me. I don't think that if I swear, God will turn into the Monopoly guy and say, "Do not pass go. Do not collect $200," and send me straight to hell. I just know this: nothing about my foul language brought me closer to Christ. No swear word I've ever used portrays that I am a child of God and that I believe that you are a child of God too. No Christian wants to feel ashamed to acknowledge their faith, and I will never forget that sickening feeling I felt when that woman on the plane asked me, "Are you Mormon?" For me, being a *witness* of God at *all* times and in *all* things and in *all* places means I need to change my language.

I wish I could say it's been easy for me to change my language. At first I would say, I'm not cussing anymore, then when I failed miserably at that, I'd say I'm not going to cuss as much. Sometimes I'd say forget it; I don't even need to change. Shoot, I'm a grown woman. My mama can't tell me what to do!

One New Year, I got serious about changing my language. From past experience I knew I needed all the help I could get, so I asked Sistas in Zion Radio listeners to call and write in with tips for keeping resolutions. One caller gave a suggestion that has shaped the entire way I now approach New Year's resolutions. She said to take your resolutions in small doses, such as a week at a time, and then reward yourself for keeping your resolution for that week. Her advice really stuck with me, and so I decided that what I really wanted to form were good habits. There's this saying out there that it takes twenty-one days to form a habit. Whether it's true or not, that seemed like a good time frame for me. I wrote my resolutions down and worked on one of them for twenty-one days. If I made it, then I'd start the next one. If not, I'd spend some more time on the first resolution

I started with no swearing. At first I really had to remind myself of my goal, and sometimes I had to bite my tongue and choose to say nothing at all because I sure didn't have anything nice to say. You know I'm hardheaded and change doesn't come easy for me, so I had to pray, fast, and go to the temple, but praise the Lord, I was able to reach my goal of twenty-one days swear free. I know some of you think it's not special, but in years past I've had to start over within hours of ringing in the New Year. It feels great that cussing isn't a habit anymore, and now when a child of God cuts me off in traffic, I try to remember: Change ain't easy, but it sure is worth it.

No Longer Language Languished,

Zandra

LOVE LETTING GO

Change isn't only about correcting things that we are doing; sometimes we need to make a change so that we can be restored from things that have happened. Restoration takes place when we decide to take control of our lives by being willing to go through the process of moving forward to transform our old selves into the new person we desire to become.

This can be a daunting task when we are trying to move on from negative experiences that we have no control over, especially if someone else causes the turmoil. Getting hurt by another person can take a piece of us, so we begin grasping for anything we can cling to so we can replace what they stole and feel in control again. What's usually right within reach is anger, shame, frustration, pain, guilt, and the list goes on. We may even cry out, "I didn't ask for any of this, so why am I the one that has to do all of this work now?" But what we are failing to realize is that hanging on takes much more strength than letting go.

Remember P.E. class back in the day? When we had all that physical education testing? The pull-up bars could be a beast! Some teachers would have you pull up and then hold at the top while they timed how long you could maintain that position. All of our energy and strength was spent in holding onto the bar. At some point we would tire, our muscles would start to ache, and we began to long for relief. When we could bear it no longer, we would let go. Holding on to negative emotions does exactly the opposite of what we are trying so hard to achieve. Instead of being in control, we are now being controlled. You know what ends up happening when we want control but our emotions want to run things? A fight happens, that's what, and the opponent is our self. And just like in gym class, if we stop fighting to hold on and instead release our grip on what is barring us, we begin to gain relief.

We've all heard the saying, "If you love something, set it free. If it comes back to you, it's yours, and if it doesn't, it never was." Music, love letters, and movies will have us thinking that letting go is only about romantic love and that the best part of letting go is getting it back. But when we are talking about healing and wholeness, ain't nobody got time for back! What we want is to move forward, and we don't want none of that mess back. If you let go of the guilt and pain of a situation, don't do what the love songs say and hope it comes back. Nobody loves being an emotional wreck. We don't hold on to anguish because we love it. We hold on because we're forgetting to love ourselves. So in the end, just like Jesus told us, everything really does boil down to love.

Sometimes when we've been fighting with ourselves for a while, it's hard to just kiss and make up. If we don't know where or how to begin loving ourselves, we need look no further than the Lord and trust that He is going to handle the situation better than we can. And yes, it is often easier said than done. There are plenty of times when we beg Jesus to take the wheel, but then some of us (and we know who we are) swat His hand away every time He reaches for it. Elder Dieter F. Uchtdorf said, "When it comes to hating, gossiping, ignoring, ridiculing, holding grudges, or wanting to cause harm, please apply the following: Stop it!" (*Ensign*, May 2012, 75).

Y'all know that in the uncut, urban-translation version Elder Uchtdorf probably said, "Asking Jesus to take the wheel, then swatting His hand away—STOP IT!" We could be wrong, but we'll probably make a printable attributing the quote to him and put it up on Pinterest anyway, 'cause once you pin it, it basically becomes true. Don't quote us on that, though. The point is, if letting go was easy, it wouldn't be hard. Let go and let Him take over. You're in great hands. Don't assume it will be easy, but rest assured, it will be effective.

Can I Get an Amen?

Tamu and Zandra

FIGHTING FORGIVENESS

From Tamu's Diary:

I was at the mall waiting for my father to pick me up, and the last thing I remember hearing was "My name is DJ, 'itch." My ear rang. I saw flashes of bright orange and red lights. I didn't know if I was spinning or the ground underneath me was spinning, but something was moving. I was disoriented and confused.

By the time my father arrived, I had lost control of my mouth and speaking had become difficult. For no reason at all, I was drooling and shaking. I didn't even notice that my nose was bleeding until the officer who had been called to the scene tilted my head back. Pain vibrated through my face and neck, and the ringing in my ear was overwhelming. I looked for my father, who was still speaking to one of the officers. The police told us that they could only ticket DJ because he was a minor. I had been assaulted! I was humiliated. Finally the tears that had been burning my eyes arrived.

As my father drove me to the hospital to confirm what the EMTs had already told me—I had a broken nose and dislocated jaw—he tried to convince me that I would be all right. If I hadn't been in so much pain, I might have yelled at my dad, "No! I'm not okay! I'm never going to be all right! I'm black AND I'm a girl!" I'd learned that night I couldn't protect myself, and if I couldn't, who could?

Time is not a healer of all things. I had serious anxiety every time I thought about running into DJ. Six months later, when he walked by me in the mall, he didn't even recognize me. But my heart felt like it was going to leap out of my chest, and I started shaking.

My friend Ryan walked over to DJ and said, "So, you like to hit girls?"

DJ tried to maneuver his way out of Ryan's grip but couldn't. He was weak. He had punched me in the face, but he didn't even try to defend himself against someone stronger than he was. For the first time since the incident, I felt vindicated!

Almost a year later, some friends and I were waiting in line at the county fair for a corndog. I heard someone call out, "DJ, do you want something to drink too?"

I froze. I turned to see DJ standing a few feet away with some girls. My friend didn't utter a word. He just ran over and hit DJ so hard it knocked him off his feet. DJ sat on the ground, looking dazed and confused. I felt like I should feel sad, but I didn't.

As we walked away, my friend said to me, "Now you're safe!"

I didn't feel safe. Now I feared retaliation, one more thing that added to my anxiety. Six weeks later opportunity presented itself, and I decided to leave home and finish high school in another state.

The summer I turned nineteen, I moved back home, and my cousins threw me a get-together (yep, it was a party). When I walked into the living room, the only face I saw was DJ's. There he was, sitting on my sofa and eating my food! When my cousin saw me, she asked what was wrong. I told her, and she could barely remember the incident. Had it happened so long ago that I was the only person who remembered that once upon a time I got punched in the face and had my jaw dislocated and my nose broken?

I repeated, "That's the guy that punched me in the face."

When the commotion cleared, my uncle emerged from the kitchen. Pointing to me, he said to DJ, "This girl has been traumatized for years. She's been afraid to leave the house alone for fear she might run into you! Look at her! Do you remember punching her in the face?"

DJ, who now referred to himself as Derek, didn't answer. He just said to the friend that had invited him that he was ready to leave.

My uncle told me to hit him in the face.

Derek looked at me and said, "I'm not just gon' let somebody hit me!"

Now, I knew that wasn't true because I had seen him get hit on more than one occasion and do nothing about it.

I balled up my fist and landed a blow right on DJ's jaw. My uncle asked me if I wanted to hit him again.

I told him I didn't.

"Does this even things out?" my uncle asked me.

I told him it did.

Later I lay in bed thinking about DJ and our interactions over the last three years. I had let what happened to me define who I was and how I lived my life. That night, I realized that I wanted to be more than just the girl that got her jaw dislocated and her nose broken. I wanted to move on and experience life just like everyone else had.

A few months after I'd gotten hit, my father told me, "You just gotta decide to let it go." At last I understood. Mentally, I needed to allow DJ to grow up, because every time I saw him it took me back to the night that it happened. I was ready to let go. It was time for me to move on, time for me to allow myself to heal. But who was going to show me how to let it go? Who was going to help me heal?

I spoke to God and told Him I was ready to let go of the grudge I'd been carrying against DJ. I told Him I was ready to feel better about myself and the people around me. I grabbed my scriptures and opened them up to a page that had nothing to do with my situation. I closed the scriptures and opened them two more times before ending up at Romans 11:36. It says, "For of him, and through him, and to him, are all things . . . be glory forever." I reflected on the many times I'd seen DJ in the past. My behavior towards him had not been a testimony of God's glory in my life.

While I was thinking about that scripture, I decided to see what Romans 12 was about. When I got to verse 19, I knew that God was letting me know that if I would let it go, He would take it up for me. "Dearly beloved, avenge not yourselves, but rather give place unto wrath: for it is written, Vengeance is mine; I will repay, saith the Lord." Not only did He have my back but He had my back with a vengeance!

I was so caught up trying to make sure that DJ learned his lesson that I kept missing the lesson(s) God was trying to teach me. I was looking to everybody except the Savior to right the wrong I had suffered. DJ was probably never going to apologize to me for what he had done, and I needed to accept that.

At some point the situation had gotten flipped. I was no longer the victim but the one responsible for DJ being victimized. I had suffered, and I wanted to see DJ suffer. I wanted his world to be just as shaken as mine had been.

Once I realized God could make me whole, the process of giving my fear and hurt to Him made sense. When Jesus was on the cross, He said, "Forgive them, Father, for they know not what they do." This struck a chord with me, because it taught me that letting go wasn't a sign of weakness. It takes real strength to let go. Letting go isn't about winning or losing. Letting go means living in God's promise.

As part of my life's journey, I've continued to learn from this story. I've allowed myself to embrace the idea that the Savior is my protector.

Still a Work in Progress,

Tamu

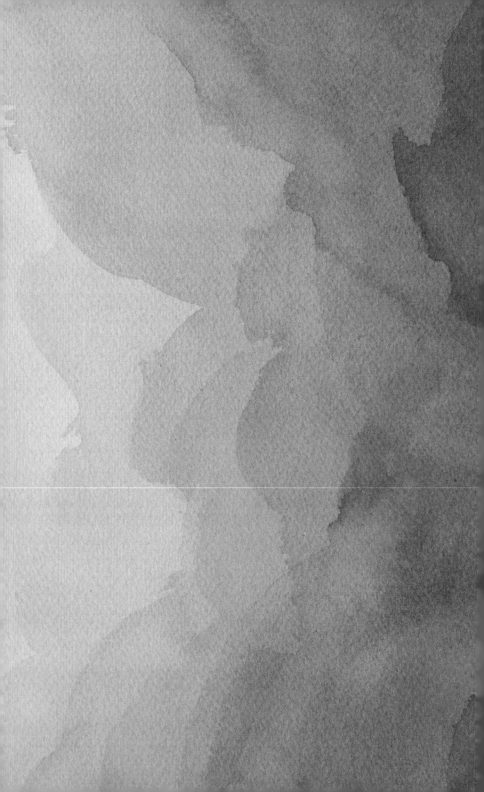

CHAPTER 6

FRIENDS AND FAMILY DISCOUNT

> Make sure you know the difference between a friends and family discount and discounting your friends and family.

DYSFUNCTIONAL FAMILIES ARE FOREVER

From Zandra's Diary:

"Raise your hand if you have a dysfunctional family." I threw my hand up as high as it could reach. I was watching some talk show—Ricki Lake, Oprah, Sally Jessy Raphael, I don't really remember which one—but it was the first time I'd heard someone use the phrase "dysfunctional family." I just knew they were talking about my crazy family tree and me. As a kid, I remember feeling like my family was so abnormal. Why couldn't we be "normal," like *Leave It to Beaver* families?

The scriptures are a place where I have always received comfort, and as I searched them with family on my mind, I started paying attention to all the families in them.

Most of the families in the scriptures don't look a thing like the families I see on television or the real-life families that seem so "perfect" to me. And the more I read, the more I saw that it wasn't just the families in the scriptures that weren't perfect. It was other relationships as well.

Between Cain, Abel, and Joseph's technicolor dream coat, it would seem that we have enough scriptural drama to last us a lifetime. Basically, every type of relationship scenario is covered in the scriptures, but apparently we would rather learn it from the *The Bachelor*. Some of you are thinking those relationships are so old and dusty they can't possibly apply to us today. Wrong. It's the same story, different people, and God has already shown us how to work it out. So what type of relationship you wanna know about?

Let's start with Mary. Even our Savior's family was not what society would consider typical. Those little girls on MTV's *Teen Mom* think they have it hard. Try being engaged, pregnant, and having to tell people that God is the baby daddy. Mary then marries Joseph, and now Joseph is raising the Son of God. Is that a "normal" family? Um, I think not, but as a person who comes from a blended family, I think it's comforting to know that the Savior did too.

Relationships have been intricate since Adam and Eve. I can't even blame it on their arranged marriage, because there wasn't anyone else for them to be interested in, and breaking up wasn't really an option. Can you even imagine Adam storming into the garden and yelling, "Eve, it's over, and I want my rib back!" Today they'd be tied up in court with community property issues forever. Yes, even at their genesis (pun SO intended!), relationships proved that they would require work.

Remember Joseph of Egypt? His daddy had a favorite son—he gave Joseph that fly technicolor dream coat and didn't get one for any of his other kids. Anyway, his brothers were so sick of the favorite son that they sold him into slavery. Now that is messed up. They took sibling rivalry to a whole 'nother level! But don't worry. Joseph overcame that situation and went on to do things so great that Donny Osmond portrayed him in a play. Now you know God has delivered you when your life story ends up in the Bible and on Broadway.

And because one dysfunctional family is never enough, we can't forget about Abraham's family feud that began when his wife got jealous of her stepson. Talk about baby mama drama. Then there's Lot with his salty wife. Doctors are always trying to tell people that too much salt can kill you, but (like some folks I know), Lot had a spouse that didn't like to listen.

And don't even get me started on marriage problems. King David was up on the housetop long before Santa Claus, except instead of delivering presents, he was up there creepin', peepin', and cheatin'. And as if that wasn't wrong enough, when he got Bathsheba pregnant, David was all about the cover-up.

If you are dating, I bet you don't have anything on Samson and Delilah's off-the-chain love affair! If ever there was a reason to run from unhealthy relationships, that is it. Before Delilah was even in the picture, Samson was gaga for a different girl, but when his fiancée's daddy forbade her to marry him, he was so distraught that he became an arsonist. The dude was running around burning stuff down to the ground! Then he ended up in a rebound relationship with Delilah, and let's just say their story could be on an episode of *Snapped*.

Not to worry if you're a single Saint. God's got you, too. Remember Martha and Mary? Those two sisters got stuck in the friend zone big time. We feel their pain—plenty of "boy" friends but no "boyfriend." When teenagers tell me that the scriptures are boring, but they're busy watching *Gossip Girl*, I sure don't understand. Daniel had to face a bully bigger than anybody they are watching on television. Even the Rock wouldn't have been able to handle what Goliath was cooking. Shadrach, Meshach, and Abednego were young men who were unwilling to shake their standards just to fit in, and unlike with our own teenage dilemmas, they faced a whole lot more than unpopularity. They were put in a fiery furnace for choosing not to keep up with the Kardashians.

Look, y'all, the more I prayed to God about my family, the more He pointed out the relationship dynamics going on in the scriptures. People were killing each other, going to jail, and selling folks out. Then I began to think. Why are these the families that are in the scriptures? Why are these the relationships that God wants us to know? He could have put picture-perfect people on these pages, but instead He kept it real. I needed to learn that families aren't perfect, and despite what I thought I saw at the neighbor's house, they never were. God wanted me to know that my family is not so different after all. You know what story isn't in the scriptures? The one where Jesus is worried about what other people might think about His mama or where He was wishing He was an only child like his cousin John the Baptist. So maybe instead of asking God to fix my family, I needed to have a little more faith in family. No, a family story that begins with a miraculous conception is not the most ordinary. But just as God placed the Savior in the ideal family for Him, my family is where God put me, and it's where He put me for a reason.

I don't just read God's word 'cause I'm looking for scripture soap operas. I search the scriptures because I know there is something the Lord wants me to know and the pages may hold the answer to a fervent prayer of mine. Today, the first place I look is in the scriptures when I feel like something dysfunctional is happening in my life. I go there and say, "Let me see if somebody has already gone through this. Let me see if I can learn something from a family in the scriptures that will help me with my plight." And it's all in there. And unlike in those made-for-television families, the relationship dilemmas in the scriptures are not solved in a thirty-to-sixty-minute time frame interrupted by paid advertising. Nope, they were solved with tools that we all have access to, such as prayer, faith, and trust in the Lord. So the next time you're looking for relationship advice, call on Jesus before you call Dr. Phil.

Dysfunction Junction,

Zandra

FRIENDS AND FAMILY DISCOUNT

MAMA GEORGIA SCROOGED ME

From Tamu's Diary:

It was a few days after Christmas, and I saw my friends Amelia and Rachel riding along outside on their brand-new beach cruisers they had just received for the holiday. I went outside and stood at the edge of my front yard, and they rode over to chat. A few minutes into our conversation, my biological mother (not my mama, Susie) walked outside and came over to us.

I innocently said to her, "Mom, do you see Amelia and Rachel's links?" (referring to the 14-karat gold link necklaces they were sporting, which were very popular at the time). "I want one just like this one," I said, pointing to the link around Amelia's neck.

My mom looked at the necklace and then back at my big brown twelve-year-old eyes. "Well, did their mothers just get out of prison?"

My heart sank and my face flushed. Let me just tell you that in my life up to that point, nothing could have prepared me for that response. There were plenty of responses that I could have handled, like "Sure, that's something we can work towards" or "Well, maybe if you save up your money," or even the standard black mama are-you-serious-right-now? look accompanied by "Do you have some gold link chain money?"

But she didn't say any of those things. Instead she asked me, outside, on the street, in front of my friends, if their moms had just gotten out of prison, and it wasn't a rhetorical question, either. She was staring at me, waiting for me to answer her. At that moment a scripture that I had heard my uncle preach on a million times popped into my head. Are you familiar with Deuteronomy 5:16? "Honour thy father and thy mother, as the Lord thy God hath commanded thee; that thy days may be prolonged, and that it may go well with thee, in the land which the Lord thy God giveth thee."

I didn't know how to respond to my biological mother because what I wanted to say was not just disrespectful. It was mean. My mom didn't raise me; she was only thirteen years old when she had me. My first memories of parents were of my grandparents. I've always known that my mom was my mother, though. I call my mother Mom and my grandparents Mama and Daddy. As a matter of fact, as I let you in on a little of the diary that is my life, you should know that most of the time when I'm referring to my parents, I'm actually talking about my grandparents because they are the ones who parented me. So when my mom said

FRIENDS AND FAMILY DISCOUNT

what she said, I wanted to tell her in the brattiest voice that my twelve-year-old self could muster that she wasn't even my real mother and that I was going to ask Mama and Daddy to buy me a 14-karat gold link. However, I knew that if I said that, not only would I not be honoring my mother but my days would not be prolonged. They would most definitely be shortened instead.

I hadn't ever seen any of the kids in my neighborhood snap on their parents successfully, and I sure wasn't about to be the butt of the story that got shared from generation to generation of the girl that got beat down for talking crazy to her mother, the mother that she already knew was 5150.*

Anyway, when my uncle would share that particular scripture in his sermons, he made it seem like if you disrespected your parents, you would just fall over and die. I wasn't entirely sold on it because although I lived in a black neighborhood, I attended a predominantly white school, where I'd witnessed a couple of kids snapping on their parents and *they* didn't die. But I knew from experience that my reality and their reality were two completely different things.

> ✱ Related to the police code for a person who is acting crazy.

As I stood there with my mother looking at me, waiting for my response, my mind continued to race. I began to think about school and what would happen when I returned after the Christmas break and faced all my peers who were bound to find out that my biomother hadn't really been on a humanitarian mission, as I had told them, but had actually just returned from a bid in the joint.*

That scripture, honor thy father and thy mother, I hated it! I had always hated it. Every time I'd heard my uncle preach it, I'd think *false*! How was I supposed to honor a father that wasn't in my life? How was I supposed to honor a mother that was in prison? It didn't matter that she went to prison for self-defense. How was I supposed to honor two people who didn't even know who I was? Nope, Uncle, that's a false scripture that doesn't apply to me. At least, that's what I always thought when he would bring it up in a sermon. I especially didn't feel like honoring my mother after she announced to my friends that she was an ex-con. There was nothing honorable about that.

While I was caught up in my thoughts having my "Save me, Lord, save me" moment, my mother got tired of waiting for me to answer her question. Because she hadn't

✽ Time in jail or prison.

embarrassed me enough, she turned to Amelia and Rachel and asked, "Have y'all's parents ever been locked up?"

They were still in shock from her question to me but managed to squeak out a "No, ma'am" in unison.

"Well, good for y'all. That's why your parents can buy you such nice gifts," my mother said. Then she looked me dead in the face like she was mad at me for something, turned her back on me, and walked away.

I didn't know what to say to my friends, and I couldn't think of any response adequate to fix the situation. Amelia and Rachel stared at my mother and then looked at each other as if trying to make sure they had both witnessed the same thing. They seemed to reach a silent agreement that they had indeed just heard my mother say that she had been in prison and not wherever I had lied to them and said she was. They then both looked at me. I can only imagine what my facial expression must have been, but their eyes were big and full of all types of questions that I wasn't even going to pretend to answer.

As I looked back at my mother as she strolled into the house, a sense of betrayal overcame me, and tears of shame began to stream down my face. My mother knew that I had lied to my friends about where she had been for the past few years, and she knew why. Most of my friends knew that I lived with my grandparents, and they often asked me about my real parents. I would make up all kinds of stories to cover up the fact that I didn't really know a whole lot about my father (he was fifteen years old when I was born) and that my mother was in the California Institution for Women. I had once been watching the television show *MASH* and saw that someone was on a humanitarian mission for the military. After asking my mama (the one who raised me) what it was, I decided to run with it. It seemed like a noble and respectable reason for my biomother to be missing in action.

So that had been my most recent story, my mother was in the military and away on some sort of humanitarian mission. I would always add, "Besides, my grandparents are my real parents; I've always lived with them because my mom had me when she was very young." I figured there wasn't any sense in lying about everything. Plus when friends would meet my mother for the first time, they were always shocked at how petite she was and how young she looked, so adding a little of the truth curbed that some. Much like the slogan for Las Vegas, my parents had a slogan: "What happens in this house, stays in this house." Well, clearly, my mother didn't get that memo, or she'd forgotten it while she was locked up. She had broken the code and my heart, and she didn't seem to care at all.

I did everything I could to avoid seeing or talking to Amelia or Rachel for the rest of the Christmas break. Since I was avoiding all people even remotely close to my age, I decided to visit my friend Thelma Tucker. Thelma was an older lady in my neighborhood. I met her when I was five, and I had been visiting her ever since. She referred to me as Li'l Dennis the Menace (I didn't figure out what she meant by that until I was much older). I was visiting with Miz Tucker, sitting at her kitchen table and watching through the window, when we saw Amelia and Rachel ride by on their beach cruisers. Miz Tucker asked why I was sitting up in the house with her instead of spending time with my girlfriends. Miz Tucker was one of my only friends who actually knew the truth about where my mother had been the last few years. We hadn't ever spoken about it, but she attended the same church as my mother's ex-mother-in-law, who had asked the congregation to pray for her son after my mother stabbed him. Even though Miz Tucker knew my mother had been in prison, she pretended to be shocked and was very empathetic when I laid out the ordeal of what my mother had done to me in front of my friends who were riding past her window. She comforted me as best she could without talking bad about my mother. I told Miz Tucker how I hated the scripture about honoring thy father and mother, and how it must certainly not apply to little girls and boys like me who had less than honorable parents, and how I was mortified to go back to school because now everyone would know where my mother had really been.

Miz Tucker looked at me, visibly shocked by my attitude. "You know, one of the things that I respect most about you is that you seem to have high standards for yourself," she said. "People that trust God don't need to fear men or what men have to say. I always thought that you were bold. You can't look at these kids and other people and measure your li'l life according to them. God expects for you to measure things according to His standards. Do you know what a standard is?"

I must have been looking at her with a blank stare because she said, "Naw, you don't know, 'cause if you did you wouldn't be looking at me with that blank look on ya face."

Now, some of the world was shocked when they got introduced to the realness of Tyler Perry's Madea. They thought that she was nothing but a refreshingly honest fictional character. Well, not to me or the folks I grew up with. We think Tyler Perry is brilliant for the way he has celebrated and brought notice to older black women. I know lots of Madeas, and Miz Tucker was one of them. They are the ones that hold together the urban neighborhoods like the one I grew up in.

Miz Tucker explained to me that a standard was much like something set up as a rule or model that other things like it are compared to. "Do you understand what I'm saying?"

I must've still had a blank look on my face because she continued on. "Do you know what *measure* means?"

I tried to look excited, and it must have worked because she said, "Don't measure yourself according to your friends or nobody else's standards. You have to look at God's word." She paused. "Do you know what God's word is?"

I couldn't believe she had asked me that question. Of course I knew what God's word was! "Yes, ma'am."

She could tell I was annoyed. "Look, baby, I'm just making sure. I don't know how deep your relationship with God goes. You've got to look at God's word to measure how you are supposed to live your life."

Miz Tucker didn't see my Deuteronomy dilemma as an issue. She told me I would have to come to terms with what it meant to honor my parents and do so according to the standards I needed to set for myself. During our conversation, she said many things that have affected my life, like how I needed to live according to the Lord's standards. She also told me that we all have people we love who have made mistakes. Sometimes those mistakes are small ones that affect a few people, and sometimes they are big mistakes that affect a lot of people. "Do you understand me?"

I nodded.

She took a sip of her coffee and continued. "Baby, if people are going to judge you for something that was beyond your control, you don't want those people in your life anyway! Your mother did what she did, and that didn't have a thing to do with you. Do you know what I'm saying?"

By this time I was crying. The more I tried to control it, the more I made that ugly sniffling sound. So, finally, I just nodded.

Miz Tucker took a long sip of her coffee. "I know it's hard, but you only got one mama." She winked. "Well, you're lucky. You got a big mama and a li'l mama. But in reality you have one mama, and if you decide to forgive her for her shortcomings now, it will save you a lot of stress and heartache in the future. Trust me, baby. Forgive her, and keep forgiving her. It's what the Good Book tells us we need to do. We are commanded to forgive those who trespass against us; it's more for us than it is for them. And when those kids at school start acting silly and teasing you, you need to forgive them, too! You know better than them. You're a good girl with a good heart!"

Why is it when old people want you to do something they compliment you? We know right then they are trying to get us to do something that we don't really want to do. I heard what Miz Tucker was saying, but I wasn't listening to her anymore. She must've slipped some brandy into that coffee she was sipping. Hey, it had been known to happen. Umm, so not only did I have to honor my parents but I had to forgive everybody else, too?

I was too young to fully understand the wisdom that Miz Tucker had imparted on me that evening. As I got older, I often thought about our conversations, especially that one. Ever since the Lord saw fit to give me that lesson, I have tried to focus more on the eternal nature of things when I'm in a situation where I know the world will want to measure me to their standards and not my own.

My friends did blab about my mother announcing to them that she had gone to prison. I did wish that the earth would open up and swallow me, but it didn't—obviously!

The kids at school eventually forgot or just stopped talking about it. I made up with Amelia and Rachel. They forgave me for lying to them about the whereabouts of my mother, and I forgave them for telling everyone. I don't even want to imagine how wrecked my life would have been if Facebook and text messaging had been around at that time. I sometimes have moments when I remember hurtful things that have happened along the way, but I did learn to let go of the hurt and forgive my mother.

A friend once explained dealing with painful relationships in terms of justice versus mercy. Sometimes the world might require justice because according to the law it is the only true punishment. However, when we make mistakes, we want someone to show us mercy in their judgment towards us. I decided to extend mercy to my mother for the mistakes she had made. I know that she isn't the mother she had hoped to be; I know she has regrets that she doesn't share with me. If I had the power to trade my life for someone else's or trade my family, I wouldn't (unless I could be a Gates, as in daughter of Bill and Melinda Gates . . . I'm playin'!). Honestly, I wouldn't trade my life for anyone else's. I am the person I am today because of the life I have lived and the people who were a part of my village.

Miz Tucker was right. I did come to terms with the scripture in Deuteronomy. I know as long as I am living a Christ-centered life, I am bringing honor to my biological parents, my mama and daddy, and my heavenly parents as well.

Still Learning to Honor,

Tamu

MISERY LOVES COMPANY

From Zandra's Diary:

When my parents decided to move our family from Atlanta, Georgia, to Salt Lake City, Utah, just as I started high school, I can tell you right now that to say I was not happy is an understatement. I immediately started praying to make my parents abort their mission. Except for the siblings who were too young to tell the difference between crossing the street and crossing the Mississippi, not one of us was happy. When it seemed my prayers would be futile, I stayed unhappy and added mad to my repertoire.

Among the many things my parents had told us to get us to soften up about our cross-country adventure, I was promised I would have my own room. I had grown up in a small, two-bedroom, one-bath home with an attic. While the move was traumatizing, the thought of not having to share a room with five other people made me stop mean muggin' my parents for a solid twenty-four hours. After that I went back to being mad.

Our new home had only four bedrooms, but after coming from the attic, we thought our modest place was palatial. Having my own room was everything I had hoped it would be. I could go in, close the door (but not lock it; my mama and daddy say lockin' doors is for people who pay some bills up in this house), and ignore everybody, especially the ones who were responsible for my miserable existence in the desert.

Once I was in Utah, I nonstop asked God to send me back to Atlanta, and when my father decided that I should attend EFY (Especially for Youth), a week-long Church summer camp, I felt that my prayers were finally answered. I just knew I was headed to Georgia for this EFY, whatever it was. Now all I had to do was "accidentally" miss my flight back to Utah, secretly live with my friend Jazzy, and finally put a smile on my face.

But no, camp was in some place called Provo at some college called Brigham Young University. Look, after I got a map and saw that Provo was not across the Mississippi but instead around some place that folks in Utah called the Point of the Mountain, I was not interested. I put my li'l teenage foot down and said too bad, so sad, I'm not going.

On the way to dropping me off at EFY in Provo, Utah (are y'all shocked that I was sitting in a station wagon on my way to Provo? You know that foot I put down a li'l earlier? I really should have been thanking Jesus that my parents didn't make me use it to run to Provo), my dad stopped by the bank and told me to go in there and withdraw some money from my account. I looked at him like he was crazy, and when he told me the dollar amount, I knew he was. I got bold and asked him what the money was for. To pay for EFY, he said. I nearly hit the roof of that Brady Bunch look-a-like wagon. "You expect me to drop that kind of cash to go to a camp that I don't even want to attend?" I said incredulously.

I kid you not, this man was serious! After a heated argument and an agreement that he would reimburse me half the cost of the camp, I went inside the bank to grudgingly withdraw my hard-to-come-by, hard-earned money. (If anybody wants to know what to get me for my birthday, half the cost of EFY, which I am still waiting for, is cool.)

By the time I got to the BYU campus I looked like the epitome of a mad black Latter-day Saint! And since I couldn't get blacker or more like a Latter-day Saint with each passing second and with every word spoken to me, I just got madder.

First of all, not only did I have to pay for EFY but I had no idea what it was—and neither did my parents. Somebody probably said, "I'm sending Sara to EFY," and my daddy was like, "So what? I'm sending my daughter to EFY too. You ain't special." And just like that my li'l behind was in Provo, ill-prepared to spend a week at camp that was costing me a good chunk of cheddar.

When we got to registration, the perky check-in woman asked me if I was excited. I looked right at her and told her no, I was not excited. And when she told me I was going to have a great time, I said, "I doubt it."

My dad gave me that look like, "Have you lost your ever-lovin' mind?" and I shot him back that you-owe-me-money look. I was perfectly aware that the only reason I was getting away with this outlandish behavior was because Dad was trying to spare all these Church folk from seeing me meet Jesus.

When I walked into the dorm room I would be staying in, to my utter dismay I realized I was going to have a roommate, even though she wasn't in the room at the moment. See, the room was identical on both sides: a closet, followed by a bunk bed followed by a desk. The right side of the room was completely bare, with just the furnishings and some bedding, but the left side of the room looked like a Sweet Valley High book had exploded all over it. There were posters on the wall, a bright pink telephone, every hair tool, cosmetic product, and perfume known to womankind organized neatly on the desk, framed family photos, brightly colored custom bedding, fuzzy throw pillows and stuffed animals. A peek into the closet showed more clothes and shoes than I even owned.

After bidding a grumpy adieu to my pops, I lay down on the bottom bunk on my side of the room, which with the contrasting décor on the left looked even more like a jail cell. Which was fitting, because I sure did feel trapped. Just as I was dozing off, I heard a scream. I jumped up to assess whether I needed to fight or flee. Standing in front of me was a blonde-haired girl.

"OH MY GOSH!" she said. "I'm so glad you're here. I thought you weren't coming. My friend Chelsea was supposed to room with me, but her parents decided to take the family to Hawaii. I didn't want to room by myself and when I got here they said that I had been assigned a roomie, but no one ever showed up, so I went out to tell registration . . ."

That's when I tuned her out and lay back down on the bed and closed my eyes.

"So where's all your stuff? Let me help you decorate your side of the room."

I tuned her back in because she had plopped down beside me on the bed and continued the conversation without skipping a beat.

"OH MY GOSH! I haven't even introduced myself," she said. "I'm Tiffani, with an I, not a Y, oh and I already know who you are because when I went down to registration the third time to tell them my roommate still hadn't shown up I asked for your name so I could check around and see if you accidentally went to the wrong room. If you don't have stuff to decorate your side of the room don't worry, I brought tons of extra stuff, this is my second year at EFY, it's so fun, but I'm going to miss my dog, she's so cute and my boyfriend, but we're on a break for the summer, but we still like love each other 'cause we're best friends, we're taking the summer to figure some stuff out and then we'll get back together when school starts 'cause we love each other so much. Have you looked at the schedule? I like already know all the classes I want to take, I hope we get a really cool counselor..."

Y'all, I put this on everything,* she then popped up from the bed, did a cartwheel in the middle of the room, squealed, sat back down, gave me a hug, and went right back on talking. "OH MY GOSH! I can't wait to get started, there are so many cute guys here..."

> * I promise I'm not lying.

This was going to be a loooong week!

That night I prayed that God would help me get something out of EFY and keep me safe from Tiffani-with-an-i. You know how you meet some roommates and you are afraid that they will strangle you in your sleep? Well, I was afraid this one was going to hug, squeal, and OH MY GOSH! me to death. I told God how unhappy I was, and I pleaded with Him for a one-way ticket out of EFY and into the ATL. This was a Church camp, right? Surely God answered prayers here.

Tiffani-with-an-i, who kept me up all night playing what she called "getting to know you" games and I called "Girl, you ask too many personal questions; get up out my business" games, had informed me that the camp classes had varying degrees of popularity on a scale of "totally awesome" to "lame-o." The next morning, when it was time to head out for classes, Tiffani found me and said, "Hurry, we have to go. Come on!"

All of sudden I saw, heard, and felt the throng of running teenagers—I'm talking running like a gold medal was at stake.

"Why are we running?" I asked Tiffani as we swerved and zig-zagged to get in front of the mob.

"The classes are first come first serve, and once all the seats are taken, then you can't get into the class," she explained.

"What?" I said, coming to a full stop.

She grabbed hold of my arm and forced me to keep moving. Were we seriously running like somebody had yelled Five-O* just to get to some classes? Tiffani-with-an-i was trippin'.

By the time we got to the class, I was hot, tired, and out of breath. I don't know where Tiffani found the energy to be leaping over desks and practically fighting people for seats, but homegirl snagged us two. As we sat down, kids were still running into the classroom, and when all the chairs filled up, people started sitting on the floor.

✻ Police; from the 1970s TV cop show *Hawaii Five-O*.

Counselors came in and tried to get some of the kids to go to other classes, but kids were begging to stay.

Now I actually started to get excited. I mean, who was teaching this class? The fact that kids were basically willing to donate an organ to come to this class must mean it was somebody HUGE, maybe Michael Jackson. Finally a man I assumed was about to announce Boyz II Men, Mariah Carey, or whoever the speaker was, got up and started speaking, but he didn't introduce anybody but himself. I was flabbergasted! We had done all that running, ducking, and dodging to listen to some skinny white guy who smiled an awful lot and said his name was John Bytheway.

"Who is this guy?" I asked Tiffani.

"Duh! It's John Bytheway," she said, looking at me as if I were crazy for not knowing who he was. Kids were pulling out journals, I guess to record what this John guy was about to say. Tiffani, who had brought everything but the kitchen sink, immediately noticed that I had nothing to take notes on and slipped me a notebook and about five fancy glitter pens.

Well, I had no clue who this guy was, but I decided if all these other teenagers were willing to take notes in the summertime while school was out, then it must be good . . . and it was. He was funny, and when he talked about teenage attitudes and how we can have the power to make changes and not be miserable, I felt that even though this brotha Bytheway wasn't offering me a ticket home to Atlanta, my prayer was being answered.

When I finished my week at EFY, I felt a little better about my moving challenge, and so I went home in better spirits than I had when I arrived.

I said hi to the fam and then headed down to my room. As soon I opened the door, I knew something was amiss. For one thing, when I left there was one bed in the room, and now there was a bunk bed. There was an extra dresser in the room, and half my stuff on the shelf had been replaced with things that didn't belong to me.

I immediately ran back up the stairs and asked my mother who had changed my room.

"I did," she said, matter-of-factly.

"Why?" I asked.

"Because we needed to move your sister into the room. There are too many people in the house for you to have your own room."

I was livid! "You promised I would have my own room when we moved here!"

"And you did," she said, "but now you need to share."

I felt like someone had slapped me across the face. The one thing that had given me any peace about this whole stupid move was being taken away from me.

"I'm not sharing my room!" I told my mother and marched downstairs. I went into the room and started picking up all my sister's things and dumping them into the hallway outside the door. My sister ran upstairs to get my mother when she saw me moving her out. By the time my mother got downstairs, I had my sister's dresser barring her entry. I clearly had lost my mind but had kept enough clarity to try to preserve my life by having a barrier between my mother and me. The doorway was blocked, but I was still throwing things over the dresser and into the hallway.

"Have you lost your mind?" my mother asked me.

"Yes," I told her.

"You are going to pick up every last thing you threw into this hallway and put it back exactly where you found it," my mother told me.

I knew my life was in danger, but I ignored her and kept throwing things out of the room. All of my siblings were now standing in the hallway, all but eating popcorn and getting ready for the show. My sister whose property I was tossing, and I'm not gonna lie, also breaking, was now tryna jump into the mix too.

"Stop throwing my stuff," she yelled.

"Well, you shouldn't have put it in my room," I told her.

"Mum told me to," she yelled.

"Oh yeah?" I said. "Well, Mum told you to come home at 9 o'clock the other night, but you came home at 10 and just barely made it in the door before Mum and Dad got home to catch you."

Now my sister realized the full extent of my psychosis. I had lost my mind enough to be breaking the sibling code of honor and was liable to get everybody in the house busted. She decided she had better join our other siblings on the sidelines and just enjoy the show. My mother had given up trying to move the dresser; I had wedged it in the door in a manner that would require her to climb up and over the dresser to get leverage.

My mother told me she hoped I was good and comfortable in the room because it would be a long time before I was ever leaving it. Eventually there were no more things to throw out of the room, but I was still mad. "You and Dad tell lies," I said, being very careful not to refer to them as liars.

My mother told me I had better watch my step.

"You said I would have my own room, and now you are taking it back. If it's not a lie, then what would you call it?"

"I don't have to answer to you," my mother told me.

Just about that time we heard the door open upstairs. My father had returned home. I started to sweat a little because while the dresser had held my mother at bay, Daddy was a whole 'nother story.

"Ya betta come down here and see what kind a madness ya chile is up to!" my mother yelled to my father.

When my father came down and saw the mess in the hallway, he was shocked.

"What is going on down here?" he asked.

"You promised I would have my own room, and now you are going back on your word," I said.

"We gave you your own room for as long as we could," he said. "There are just too many people in our family for you to have your own room."

"I don't want to live here! You're taking away the one thing that was positive, and you guys did it so shadily. That's why you sent me to EFY, so you could sneak around and change the rooms!"

That night I slept on the floor with the dresser still wedged in the door. I woke up to the sound of my dad un-wedging it in the morning. I did have to pick up every last thing I threw into the hallway, and I was grounded for months.

In the weeks afterward, I couldn't act crazy with my parents because there was no longer a dresser saving my life, so I took my anger out on my sister. I refused to acknowledge that I shared a room. I ignored her if she spoke to me. I would turn off the lights when she was reading or rattle, open, slam, drop, and shake things when she was sleeping. As she tried to make her side of the room her own by hanging things up, by the time she turned around, I had taken them down and hidden them.

No matter how much I cried and prayed and begged, I felt as though God was ignoring me. He wouldn't lift my misery. Eventually being mean to my sister didn't make me feel better; it started to make me feel worse. My sister wasn't the one who had taken away my room. My sister actually didn't want to be in Utah any more than I did. I was so angry at the misery that my parents had caused me that I wasn't even paying attention to the fact that I was compounding my sister's misery by behaving like a wicked stepsister.

As I pondered my plight, I spied the EFY notebook that Tiffani-with-an-i had given me. I picked it up and read all the things that had inspired me that week. When I left EFY, I had certainly felt uplifted, but I had come home and hadn't done any of the things I had learned, so nothing had changed. Here I was praying to God to change my situation, and I wasn't even willing to put into practice the gifts He'd bestowed on me.

I eventually had to come to terms with the fact that I wasn't going home to Atlanta, and I had to stop acting like I was the only person in the house that was affected by being uprooted. I needed to learn to stop taking my anger out on others and start becoming responsible for my own happiness.

In Pursuit of Happiness,

Zandra

HOT MESS-IPE

From the moment of our existence, we were loved and knew how to love. The scriptures tell us, "We love him, because he first loved us" (1 John 4:19). It's as simple as that. God loves us, no ifs, ands, or buts about it. We don't have to do anything to receive it. He gives it freely, and He loves us first, regardless of what we do second. Sometimes we wonder how deep God's love for us is. Well, He loved us so much that He gave His Only Begotten Son, and because of His atoning sacrifice, we are all born into unearned favor.

What do we have to do to make our relationships with people as simple as our relationship with God? And who decided that relationships were going to be so complicated? We can tell you one thing. It wasn't Him. We have an idea of who it was, and why we would listen to somebody who doesn't even have a body is beyond us. God designed relationships between us and others to be simple—it has only three ingredients: He loves us, so we love Him, and when we love Him, then we love one another. That's it.

But because of a little thing called agency (which, by the way, He gave us because He loves us), we decide to take the family recipe and add a li'l spice. That's how we end up with a mess-ipe,* and some of our relationships end up too hot to handle. You know what we're talking about. After it starts boiling is when we try to turn the pot over to God. He picks up the spoon, takes a li'l taste, and asks, "Who made this? This isn't the original

> ✱ Pronounced like *recipe*. Combination of *hot mess* and *recipe*, it's a recipe for disaster.

recipe. Somebody call Colonel Sanders so I can help this chil' fix this."

God gives us opportunities to have many different types of relationships because He expects us to continue sharing and accepting love. But once we mess with the Flavor of Love, we've got to focus on getting back to basics. He gave us the perfect recipe and then provided us with counter-recipes to fix the recipe when we screw it up. God is so good.

Can I Get an Amen?

Tamu and Zandra

DESPICABLE ME

From Tamu's Diary:

I was on my way to lunch with friends, and she was standing at the light across from the bank. Her sign read, "Homeless! Please Help!!!" Despite the conversation happening around us, a friend noticed me watching the woman holding the sign. My friend said she'd noticed that more homeless people were moving into our area. She called it a sign of the times. "We are in the last days," she said.

The light changed, and we continued toward our destination. The others continued to talk about the influx of poverty in our area; there was nothing for me to contribute to the conversation. I had just done something so despicable I couldn't even believe it.

I had denied my mother. My biological mother was standing on a corner holding a sign, begging for help, and I didn't even acknowledge her. I didn't call out to her. I didn't say, "That looks like my mother." I could have at least said that. Instead, I stood there with my mouth shut and didn't say anything because, well, I was embarrassed. I was embarrassed by my mother's situation, and I felt ashamed of myself for being embarrassed. For once, I wanted to blend in; I wanted to be a regular woman, on a regular day, going to lunch with some regular folks.

The truth is, I was afraid that if my friends and coworkers discovered who my mother was before I had an opportunity to buffer or soften her story with my own niceties, not only would they judge my mother but they would judge me. I just didn't feel it would be safe to own up that the homeless woman standing at the crosswalk was my mother.

I know it's not the same, but for a second, just in that moment, I could imagine what the disciples must have felt like when they rejected Jesus. No matter how difficult and complicated my relationship with my mother was, I don't ever want to experience the shame I felt the day when I saw her in need and turned away.

Unbelievable Me,

Tamu

BRINGIN' THE PEPPER TO SALT LAKE

From Zandra's Diary:

No, moving from Georgia to Utah during high school did not a happy camper make. Well, since I wasn't planning on staying long (I hadn't given up hope of finding an underground railroad that headed south), I didn't see the need to make any friends, plus who would I be friends with? If the kids I met weren't telling me I was the first black person they had ever met in real life, then they were showing me something or other out of *National Geographic Magazine* and asking me to explain it to them. If I'd said it once, I'd said it a thousand times: The only tribe I was familiar with was A Tribe Called Quest.* I mean, I know it's Salt Lake City, but dang, could a sista not feel like she was the only pepper up in this joint?

Just like Will Smith says, parents just don't understand, and the Fresh Prince wasn't lying, not about my parents, at least. Every time I went somewhere, it was the same question: "Did you make any friends?"

> * A hip-hop group.

Really?

"Mum, I walked to the 7-Eleven. Who do you want me make friends with, a trucker?"

"Well, maybe the trucker has a daughter your age?" she said encouragingly.

All I was thinking was, "Maybe the trucker was headed to Georgia."

Every conversation ended with me letting my parents know I had plenty of friends and would be happy to kick it with them if they would only purchase me a one-way ticket home because this Georgia peach was not interested in making any friends in the Beehive State.

One Sunday, my father decided to take matters into his own hands. I can only assume he figured he hadn't quite ruined my life enough. At church, he summoned me over to him. He was standing next to a girl who looked about my age.

"This is my daughter Zandra," he said to the girl. "She doesn't have any friends."

My mouth dropped open as I looked at my father in disbelief. He turned to me. "Well, didn't you say you don't have any friends?"

"I'm not a loser," I said. "I have more than enough friends."

"Well, how come all you do is sit around at home with that forlorn look on your face?"

Wow! He was really trying to embarrass me in front of God, this girl I didn't even know, and everybody else at church. I didn't know what look he was talking about, but I know that if looks could kill, the one that was on my face at that moment was liable to turn sacrament meeting* into a funeral service.

"I never said I didn't have friends," I said.

"Oh," he said. "I could have sworn you were in need of a friend."

"Well, I'm not," I told him.

✱ Sunday church service.

"That's too bad," he said, "because I already found you one." He gestured toward the other girl. "Zandra, this is

Graciela. She needs a friend, and although you say I'm mistaken, I already told her that you were available."

The two of us just stood there looking at each other.

"Okay," he said, "so what do we do now? Do we put our hands together and do a cheer or something else to make it official?"

I gave him the most lethal glare I could muster.

He thought he was so amusing. "I don't know what girls do. I thought y'all had a ritual or had to sign a pledge or something. Well, you can do that part later then, but I know enough to know that you are supposed to be talking. Girlfriends love to talk, or do you all only do that over the phone when other people need to use it?"

I could see he wasn't going to stop. "Dad," I grumbled through gritted teeth.

"Okay, okay." He chuckled as he turned and walked away like he was the coolest cat in the chapel.

Graciela and I stood there silent for a moment, and then she said, "Your dad said you just moved here. Me too."

"You like it here?" I asked.

"No," she said. "I want to go home."

She had me at "go home." And even though her English was a little broken, I had finally found somebody who was speaking my language.

"Where'd you move from?" I asked.

"Guess," she said.

She was brown and had an accent, so I figured it was somewhere outside the U.S. "El Salvador?"

She shook her head no.

"Puerto Rico?"

No.

"Is it a Spanish-speaking country?" I asked.

She nodded.

"Dominican Republic?"

No.

"Venezuela?"

No.

"Cuba?"

She laughed. "No."

"I give up," I said.

"Mexico," she said.

"Oh," I said, "that's cool. I definitely wouldn't have guessed that."

"How come?" she asked.

"I don't know," I said. "I guess because I've never met someone from Mexico."

"You've never met a Mexican?" she asked, looking at me strangely.

I had to chuckle. "That's the same look I give folks out here when they tell me they've never met a black person before," I said.

She smiled. "Well, I've never met a person from Georgia before, so I think we're even."

And just like that, we were amigas. Graciela said if I would help her with speaking English, she would help me pass my Spanish class. It was perfect because she was helping me get A's, and the more fluent she got, the less I had to speak. If some stranger even put a hand anywhere near my head, she would be on it with a "Never touch a black girl's hair!" Graciela was quick. The next thing you knew, she'd be adding a couple of finger snaps at the end of her sentences.

Good girlfriends are more precious than gold. Even when we think we don't need anyone, God places people

FRIENDS AND FAMILY DISCOUNT

in our path because He knows we do. At the time, neither Graciela nor I thought that Utah had anything to offer us besides Jell-O, but it turns out we each found a lifelong friend in the Beehive State.

Amigas para Siempre,

Zandra

CHAPTER 7

RELATIONSHIP RECIPE

God's recipe for healthy relationships is
1 part love and 70 times 7 parts forgiveness,
so don't try to blame it on Him if your
relationships are extra salty and
gotta whole lotta beef.

RELATIONSHIP REALITY CHECK

Have you ever felt like you were in need of a reality check? Why do we get so caught up in what's happening on the front pages of the tabloids when we should really be concerned about what's happening within the four walls of the homes we live in?

With everything that we are exposed to today, sometimes we need to unplug, unload, and check ourselves. What good does it do you to know if and when Kimye are getting married if your own marriage is falling apart? Relationships are difficult enough without bringing in extra drama from somewhere else. The world will lead you to believe that if your relationship was more like that of (well, just insert your favorite celebrity or noncelebrity couple right here), then you would be happy. It's human nature to examine other people's relationships from the outside and think that's what you want too. People usually don't announce the real ugly in their relationships until it's too late and they are doing it in front of the media or in a courtroom.

It may be human nature to want to compare, but it's not the nature of God. Comparison can teach us valuable lessons that we need to learn, but it can also be detrimental to our relationships, especially if our comparison turns into coveting or becomes disruptive to our relationships or us. Just because your mother-in-law had a made-from-scratch, six-course meal on a perfectly set table by six o'clock every day doesn't mean that this should be the expectation in your marriage. When we use the relationships of others to measure our own, we are setting ourselves up for failure.

It's easy to look at what other people are doing and think that you would like to have what they have. However, you may not want to go through what they've gone through to get to where they are in their relationship. Made-for-television movies and fairy tales are exactly what they claim to be—entertainment. They aren't real life, not for most people. And basing your relationship on what you see on television will leave you praying for a commercial break.

When Beyoncé sang that love got her looking crazy in love, it sounds real cute set to music, but in our real life, crazy love is not fun, and quite frankly, downplaying the crazy can desensitize us to unhealthy and dangerous relationships. Teens aren't the only ones who create relationships so full of drama that they actually begin to think crazy is what love looks like. Adults do it too. Take it from us, madly in love does not equal crazy in love.

Can I Get an Amen?

Tamu and Zandra

DON'T SAVE THE DRAMA FOR MAMA

From Zandra's Diary:

My honey and I had a spat. I thought this was supposed to be the honeymoon stage. I don't remember what the tiff was about, but that's not even why I am telling this tale anyway. I don't know why I did it . . . probably because I now have cable for the first time in my life and I've watched one too many made-for-TV movies . . . but I digress. Well, I stormed out of the apartment mid-argument, slammed the door for good measure, sashayed to the vehicle, and peeled out of the parking lot. He had better realize that I'm a grown woman! That's why I was heading down the highway so I could go tell my mama on him. When I got to the house, I rang the doorbell, which was answered by just the person I needed right then.

"What are you doing here at this hour of the night?" my mother said.

With tears in my eyes, I squeaked out, "We had a fight."

SLAM!

I didn't say slam, and my mother didn't say slam, either. SLAM was the sound of the door slamming in my face. I stood on the stoop, dazed and confused.

"Goodnight," I heard my mother say through the door.

I was sure she was losing her mind. That was the weirdest reception I'd ever had from her. I rang the doorbell, hoping the ding-dong sound would snap her out of her psychotic break. After a minute of that, I walked around back to see if that door was unlocked. Nope. Beyond frustrated, I began to rap on the bedroom windows. Finally my little sister opened the curtains, and a big smile spread across her face when she saw that it was me.

"What are you doing here?" she asked through the glass.

"Sleeping over," I said. "Come open the front door for me."

She scurried out of her room.

What was taking her so long? I rang the doorbell incessantly; maybe it was broken. I knocked on the door. No answer. I beat on the door. Still no answer. I slumped into a sitting position on the cold front step just as bewildered as ever. After sitting for about fifteen minutes, I heard a tap on one of the front windows. I ran over and saw my little sister's head pop up in the window. She put her finger to her lips for me to be quiet.

"Mum says no matter how many times you ring the doorbell or how loud you bang on the door, if anyone in this house opens the door for you, they'll be sleeping outside too."

What? My mother really wasn't going to let me in the house and she didn't care if I slept on the stoop? Well, there was nothing my seven-year-old sister could do for me, so I told her to go to bed, and I went back to my place on the porch. I looked around at the other houses on the street. It finally dawned on me that people might have witnessed me running around the house like a crazy person and banging the door down.

Tears of shame began to stream down my face. So this is what happens when you get married? Your mother turns into a wicked stepmother and lets you sit out in the cold? A half-hour into my pity party, I heard footsteps at the front door. I jumped up and saw my mother's silhouette through the door's frosted windows. I quickly wiped the tears from my face and waited for her to unlock the door. Her hand reached forward and . . . darkness. She had turned off the porch light. I heard her walk away from the door, and then I saw the last ray of hope disappear as the light in my parents' bedroom went off. Now I was standing alone in the pitch-black night.

I contemplated sleeping on the porch just for spite, so she would feel bad in the morning, but I was already way too cold for that, and what on earth would I say to the neighbors who found me drooling on the concrete as they jogged by on their early morning run? I tucked my tail between my legs, got into my car, and drove home.

By the time I got into the bedroom, I was exhausted. I shed my street clothes and slid into the bed, trying not to wake up my husband. As soon as my head hit the pillow, though, he rolled over, put his arms around my waist, and slid me across the bed.

He snuggled next to me and asked, "How's your family?"

I was a little shocked since I hadn't told him where I was going, but determined to keep the upper hand, I replied, "Mad at you."

He sleepily chuckled.

"What's so funny about that?" I inquired.

"No, they're not," he said playfully.

I didn't know what had gotten into him, but I wasn't in the mood for fun and games. "Oh, yeah?" I snapped.

"Yeah," he said. "Your mother called me."

"What!" I exclaimed, popping into a sitting position right there in the bed. So my mother could talk, just not to me? "What did she say?"

He sat up in the bed too, and between yawns, he said, "That she wanted me to know that you were at the house and she didn't know anything about anything and neither did anyone else there, and that's the way she wanted to keep it."

"Oh," I said, lying back down.

"So did you have fun? What did you and the fam do?" he asked while snuggling back down next to me.

"Oh, nothing much. Just sat around," I said.

Then we both apologized for the night's events and drifted off to sleep.

The next morning my mother called me. You know I had an attitude, and you know she couldn't have cared less.

"Good morning," she said, all chipper.

I knew she was 'bout to act like she didn't know that I knew that we both knew that she had lost her ever-lovin' mind last night. Of course I wasn't dumb enough to say that, so instead I said a grumpy, "Morning."

She engaged me in some small talk, which was mostly her talking and me making sounds like umm, hmmm, and oh.

Eventually she said, "And about last night . . ."

Finally I was about to get an apology and explanation for last night's 5150-ness.*

"Don't you ever do that again!" she said.

"What?" I muttered in shock. I had been in shock so many times in the last twelve hours it was a miracle my heart hadn't stopped.

"You are a grown woman," she said, "and you are going to do what you want, but I don't want you ever running to me when you and your husband have a fight. Do you understand?"

* Related to the police code for a person who is acting crazy.

RELATIONSHIP RECIPE

I responded affirmatively, too stunned to do anything else.

"Nor do I want you running to your father or any of your siblings. I also suggest that you don't run to any of your friends, either."

So apparently my mother didn't want me running anywhere, which was fine by me because I don't even like running. Personally I feel like now that the underground railroad is closed, I don't have to run anymore, which is exactly what I explained to my track coach when I asked her to stop putting me down for cross-country events. I know a lot of people enjoy distance running, but I just don't see the point of me running through the woods, dirt, and streams if I'm not heading north and I'm already free.

After we sat in silence for a moment, my mother said, "Look, no marriage is perfect. You and your husband are going to have disagreements sometimes, but that's between you, your husband, and the Lord. When you're in the heat of the moment and angry, if you run off and tell everybody the personal details of your marriage, after the two of you have made up, everybody you told will still know. I don't want you to ever have to be in a situation where you tell me something about your husband that makes me angry at him, because you might get over it, but that doesn't mean

I will. And I don't ever want him to feel embarrassed in your family's home or to be around your friends because we know all his business. When we are young and in love, we like all the drama, but take all that dramatic energy and put it into your prayers, because when you have a disagreement with your husband, the only person you should be running your mouth to is Jesus."

Mum taught me a cold harsh lesson that night, and I don't want to say it because she already thinks mother knows best, but she was right. I eventually came clean to my husband and told him the truth about how my mother had actually treated me like my name was Mary and there was no room in the inn and had me camping on the front step.

After my hubs picked himself up off the floor and dried the tears of laughter from his eyes, he too acknowledged that he was grateful for my mother's wisdom.

Trying to Be a Drama-Free Me,

Zandra

RELATIONSHIP RECIPE

I'VE BEEN DECEIVED

From Tamu's Diary:

Dr. Phil, here I come! How many mistakes can parents make with their children before they end up in a book with one of their children referring to himself as "It"? If the number of mistakes is five, would that be per child or total? I'm feeling a little salty toward God, because kids should come with an instruction manual.

All right, let me tell you what happened, before I get myself even more worked up. Two days ago, I came home from work and spotted a full-sized candy bar in the middle of my bathroom floor, lying next to a pair of scissors. My inner private investigator kicked in, and I started asking questions. At the time, I had eight little kids at home, ranging in age from two to fourteen years old, and no one knew what happened? I was annoyed that they had found my Snickers stash. And I was annoyed that someone had taken a bite (did I mention that? Yeah, someone took a bite!) out of the Snickers and left it on the bathroom floor! I became even more annoyed when my attempts to crack the case of the Bathroom Snickers Bandit yielded no confessions.

That's when I decided I was going to have to do what I had to do to get the truth. I sent all the kids to their rooms and told them that when whoever had taken the Snickers was ready to confess, they were welcome to talk to me. Until then, I would be in my room getting ready to attend a family member's wedding reception, and unless the person who snuck the candy bar confessed, they were all going to stay home (don't judge me). My philosophy was, If you will steal at home, you will steal in public. Crazy, right?

There are times when people, especially parents, draw a line in the sand, which creates a personal dilemma, especially if the parents should ever need to jump back onto the other side of that line. By the time I was finished getting ready, it was time to go. I felt bad, but what could I do? I had already told my kids that if they didn't confess, they had to stay home in their rooms.

You know that saying that crazy people have crazy children? Well, clearly, I had crazy parents. If one of us kids got in trouble, we were all in trouble. I had said I was *never* going to treat my kids like that, but that was before I had kids. Having my own children has helped me develop an attitude of mercy rather than vengeance toward my parents.

As I was walking out the door, one of the girls came to me and said, "Mom, I did it. I'm the one who got the candy bar. Now can we all go to the reception?"

When I asked her why she hadn't told me earlier, she shrugged her shoulders. "I don't know," she mumbled.

I was suspicious of her confession because that particular kid would have removed all the evidence if it actually had been her. I asked her if she had really snuck into my room and got into the Snickers.

This time she said no.

I didn't know what to believe.

"Why did you say you did it, if you didn't," I demanded to know.

She told me that they (the other kids) had discussed it, and it was decided that she should confess, so she did. I was beyond frustrated at that point. So she was sent back to her room.

The next morning was Saturday. During breakfast, my husband and I spoke to the kids about taking things that didn't belong to them and what it meant to be honest. The only one confessing was the two-year-old. He had actually started confessing the day before, but I knew it couldn't be him. Not only could he not reach my Snickers stash but he didn't know how to operate scissors, especially not the adult-sized scissors that were lying on my bathroom floor. Again, there was that line in the sand I didn't want to cross.

I sent the kids back to their rooms and went about my business. They needed to learn a lesson, and I was teaching it to 'em! My husband had been unusually levelheaded, and I kind of needed him to bail me out. Usually he is my calm; however, the last time he intervened on behalf of the kids, I'm pretty sure my bark was so loud, he didn't want to experience my bite. So, he allowed me to continue on the road I was on. He later told me his thoughts were, if nothing else, the time in their rooms gave the kids a chance to read and catch up on homework.

I went about my business the rest of the morning. By lunchtime, my five-year-old had called me several times. Each time I answered the phone, I heard his tearful confession.

"Mom, I did it."

To which I would respond, "Really?"

Then he would reply, "No, the older girls said they know I'm the one who did it, so I said okay."

"So, you didn't really do it?" I would ask him.

He'd say, "No, I think Eli (the two-year-old) did it. Do I still have to go back to my room?"

As heartbreaking as it was, back to his room he was sent. Feeling that they had suffered long enough but still not wanting to cross the line that I had been foolish enough to draw in the sand, when I returned home, I gave the kids one more chance to tell me what happened.

Again, the two-year-old said, "Mommy, I have tandy!"

Before I could respond, my husband said, "Can you show me and Mommy where the candy is?" My husband lifted him out of his high chair. The kid was still in his PJs.

He ran into our bedroom, climbed up the bookshelf, reached into my candy bar stash, grabbed a candy bar, let it fall to the floor, and then climbed down. I was speechless! He then ran over to my nightstand, pulled out the scissors, took them into the bathroom, and set them on the floor. He ran back into the room and grabbed the candy bar he'd dropped. He walked back into the bathroom (by now we were all, even the kids, watching with amazement) and neatly placed the candy bar on the floor, making sure the end of the wrapper was pulled straight. He then picked up the scissors by the handles, pulled the scissors open with both hands, and carefully slid the open scissors across the straight end of the wrapper. Squeezing both hands together, he snipped the wrapper of the candy bar open. Finally, he picked up the candy bar and looked up at me, his father, and all his siblings with a big satisfied smile as he finished tearing open the wrapper. We were all shocked, but no one was more shocked than I was.

Once I realized that my two-year-old had abilities that exceeded my expectations, I felt foolish! I felt like I had been deceived! I wanted a do over. Several times over the past day and a half I had felt uncomfortable with the punishment I'd laid out for them, yet I was unwilling to yield. I thought I was teaching them a lesson but ended up learning one myself. My parents' philosophy when punishing prematurely was, "That's for something I missed or might miss." So, it's safe to say that being given an apology by my parents was very rare.

I faced my kids, who had already seemed to forget the whole ordeal. They had already started joking about it and making fun of me. I could have downplayed the situation but chose not to. They had missed out on attending a family wedding reception and the opportunity to play with friends on a Saturday, one of the last good ones of the season. I needed them to know that I was wrong, and I needed to ask for their forgiveness. Isn't it crazy how something that seems so simple can be so difficult?

Shamefaced, I explained (I had to speak loudly because they were celebrating) that being a parent didn't mean I

RELATIONSHIP RECIPE

wouldn't make mistakes and get it wrong sometimes. It meant that at times everyone could learn from the mistakes I made. I told them that I was sorry for accusing them of stealing and lying to me, and I hoped they would forgive me. They could have responded in a nasty manner, but they responded with love and grace.

I've learned, and continue to learn, that unless I see it or experience it on my own, I cannot say what someone will or won't, can or can't do! 'Cause that's how people get deceived!

A Little Shame in My Game,

Tamu

RELATIONSHIP STATUS

You want to know when the world got extra serious about relationships? In 2004. That's the year Facebook was invented. Mark Zuckerberg wasn't even in a relationship when he started throwing all of ours into a frenzy. Not only did our love lives get put on blast* but he was complicating friendships before we knew they could get complicated and

> ✱ To call somebody out in an embarrassing manner.

everybody was now your "friend." This has got kids so confused. They think that their Facebook friends are their real friends and don't even know how to have face-to-face conversations. Family life got real as well. Those immediate family members that you are pretending are distant cousins can list you as their relation and tag you in those embarrassing family photos. Speaking of getting real, now reality television is showing us "real" love, teen love, and tough love. Relationships require work, but these days with all these complexities, they require double and triple overtime. Thank goodness God is there to remind us that we shouldn't Facebook our problems. We should face them.

In this era of tweeting, pinning, and sharing, it can be hard to know the difference between being open and putting all your business out there. Here's the thing about relationships we can't ever forget: It's not just about you. A family is made of members, and not every member is going to be as open as you may be.

Years ago when we started our blog, we immediately realized that we had to be conscious and respectful about the things that we share. Yes, they are our lives, but our lives are filled with people, people we love and care about. Even as we wrote this book and chose to share lessons and personal experiences from the diaries of our lives, it was not done without careful consideration.

We can't take back what we put out there about our relationships, and just because all is forgiven on our end doesn't mean that everyone we told has forgotten. Of course there are appropriate times for sharing, but making your boo's preference for boxers or briefs your Facebook status might not be one of them. Not everything going on in our relationships is share worthy. We can tell people that our baby threw up without posting the picture.

Youth are put in the hot seat all the time for breaching their family's unwritten gag order. When the "Parents say things like" hashtag starts trending on Twitter, it definitely has us rollin', but we know some kids end up grounded. As a society, we put so much information on the Internet that we had to give the problem its own acronym, TMI—Too Much Information. The bottom line is, we gotta be careful with the TMI before our relationships end up RIP.

Can I Get an Amen?

Tamu and Zandra

DROPPIN' THE MIC

How much of our diaries did you think we were going to let you read? If we wanna stay boo'd up* and be invited to the next family reunion, we have to keep some things private. We know we just dropped a lot of knowledge on you, not only about who we are but also about who God is to us. These are just a few of the lessons we've had the opportunity to learn thus far in our lives, because you know God isn't through with us yet.

> * In a relationship.

It's not always easy learning the lessons, so y'all know it's not easy to share them, either. But one of the things we've learned is that no matter how alone we think we are in our situation, there is probably somebody out there who is going through something similar. Our hope in sharing with you our experiences and what we've learned is not to preach but to help you feel encouraged to search for and recognize your own lessons and the blessings in your life.

Every day is a blessing, and every day holds a lesson. So, what are some of the lessons you've learned? We're not trying to be all up in your business, but since you had your nose all up in our diaries, we thought we were at least cool enough with each other to be allowed to ask you a few questions. We know our real talk might be nothin' like your great-aunt Belinda's, so if you listen, you listen, and if you've figured out a better way of discovering the lessons in your life, we ain't mad at ya. We're just sharing with you what our journey of discovery has been and how we've been able to keep track of what God has taught us and all that He has given us to be grateful for.

The great thing about finding the Lord's lessons in everyday life is that God is going to keep on loving us. All we have to do is keep on living. We all have times when we think, "I can't wait for this day to be over," but that doesn't mean there wasn't a lesson of love from the Lord. God doesn't take sick days. He puts purpose and meaning in every day. It's up to us to find it.

Think of it like this. What if we told you that we were going to give you one million dollars every year for the rest of your life? Just to be clear, this is a hypothetical; you are not 'bout to find a check on the next page. So, if you're anything like us, the next thing out of your mouth would probably be, "What I gotta do to get this money?"

So here's what you have to do to get your hypothetical million dollars: FIND IT! Every day $28,000 will be waiting for you. It might be at work, your mama's house, or school; it could be anywhere. So here's the catch. (Stop acting like you didn't know there'd be a catch.) There are no days off. If you want the million dollars each year, you have to make the time every day to find the $28,000. Skip a day, and you don't get the million. Find it each day, and the reward is yours to keep.

The question we have to ask ourselves is, What value do we place on God's daily love? How dedicated are we to finding purpose in each day? How motivated are we to find what's priceless? How urgent is it to us to find peace, forgiveness, joy, and love? When we know that God has something in store for us each and every day, we can't help but be grateful.

We have been taught by good, godly people that where there is teaching, there is love, and where there is learning, there is humility and grace. As we've said before, God's love lessons are everywhere. All we have to do is look, and through His loving grace and with some humility, hopefully we will find them.

Brothas and sistas, our time has come to an end. Just remember to send the praise up as the blessings come down. God be with you till we meet again.

Can I Get an Amen?

Tamu and Zandra

SHOUT OUTS

TO THE PEOPLE WHO PUT UP WITH ME

Love, Zandra

First & foremost, I give GOD the glory.

To my boo Nicholas: I love you! Where would I be without my baby? I can see Mike Jordan from here.

To my loving parents: Mum, you are "sew" special. You brought me into this world—I'm so happy you didn't take me out. Daddy, sometimes you're right; I'm not a follower. I said sometimes.

To my bacchanal bunch: I love you all! Juliet, no matter what, you're never on the Pharcyde of my heart. Joan, when you're in my life, it's carnival. Kiss for my Nia. Cleo, I'm ready for our adventure. I'm not getting on the bike. Errol, aka "E," my best man. You grew up as the only.

SHOUT OUTS

You're welcome. Davina, me, you, DEB, Jake, and the crew. Those were good times; let's have more. Lorna, you probably think this song is about you. It is. Carolynn, aka Caca, my favorite laugh in the whole world. Sonobello. Theo, you're the best. No offense. Allana, you're gonna make it. So let it be written, so let it be done.

To my Trini-Fam: We love, we laugh, we lime.

To Karin: You and old man Watts are always there for me.

To Jasmine: From Nancy Creek to forever.

To my Vranes fam: I couldn't ask for more. Barry Manilow, John Denver, Neil Diamond . . . I pick next. Love living in a van with Braxton, Cade, Davis, Brittea, and the supertan baby on the way.

To Rayshaun, Jalyn, Maya, Isaiah, Elijah, Xeon: You see that there love? I shot it. So I could give it to you.

To Viteria, Vera, Vanna, Maykela: Aunty forever.

To Team Get Lost: You are the best finds. Take a hike!

To Diana: Mi hermana.

To Muaka MuMu: Forever grateful for the gospel for giving me my sister and sista. Can you read? I ain't impressed.

To my angels in heaven: Louise Mary Roberts, Theophilus Maynard & Sally Ball Vranes.

SHOUT OUTS

TO MY PEEPS!

From Tamu

I first give honor to God, from whom all blessings flow.

To Edna (mother): Thank you for making a difficult choice at such a young age.

To Raymond Sr. (father): Thank you for finding your way back to me!

To Aunt Rozene, Aunt Maxie-Jean, Uncle Fred & Aunt Carol, Uncle Jim Lane, Uncle Robert & Aunt Yolanda (Faye), Uncle Philip, Aunt Linda, Aunt/Sister Kimmi, Uncle Robert & Aunt Minni, Grandma Emma, Mama Cathy Stokes, and Papa Gray & Leslee. I can't remember a family occasion without us singing something. Today I sing to you: "That's family business!"

To all my Gremlins: Aboyomi, Andy, Alphonso, Leah, Lajoyce, Lateefah, Latoya, Antiea, Viteria, Vera, Vanna, Raymond Jr. & Maykela. Also them Double "O's," the rest of the Woods family, and Calwa Crew!

To my sisters & my sistas: Amanda, Fayola, Kammiko, Nichola & Shante. Ride or die.

To Alisha, Angie, Carolyn, Kendra, LaShanda, Nkoyo, Regina & Yolande: I love y'all like a fat kid loves cake, and I appreciate you more than words can say!

SHOUT OUTS

To Mama Rine for being my right and sometimes even my left hand!

To my sista from another mista, Zandra: I am forever grateful that you saw, captured, and enhanced the vision!

To all my cousins, aunts, uncles, and friends whose names escape me at this time.

To Doug & Carol Hinckley (Momz & Popz), Deanna, Sean Lamar, M. Brunner, Tom & Bonnie, Mom & Dad Olsen, Pat & Larry, Brady Family, Bybee Family, Kehl Family, Richins Family & err'body in Henefer! They say that blood is thicker than water. Well, according to this list, it ain't! Ya'll restore my hope in humanity: "We are family!"

To the Haskins Family for taking care of & feeding my kids while I wrote this book!

To Donna and the late Don Smith: Thank you for my BFFAE!

To my KIDZ—R, J, M, I, E & little X: Thanks for being patient with me, especially on the nights I was glued to the computer writing this book when I should have been glued to the stove making PB&J sandwiches.

Last but not at all least, I acknowledge my husband, lover, and very best friend, Keith Walter Smith. THANK YOU for learning how to be a cheerleader for me. Without you, "this" could not have happened.

SHOUT OUTS

FROM THE SISTAS

Without Genesis, our sistahood wouldn't be. Thank you to our Genesis family, all of you! Remember, if you came once, you are a member!

To Ruffin Bridgeforth, Darius Gray, and Eugene Orr, the O.G. presidency who had the foresight to know Genesis would be needed to nurture our souls before they even knew who we were.

To our beginning Genesis family, before we were a big enough family to meet in the chapel and we met in the Relief Society room: Balfour, Bridgeforth, Brock, Camomile, Dodds, Dudley, Gray, Hamilton, Harwell, Hawkins, Lee, McDonald, Perkins, Sheppard, Smith, Sorenson & Young.

To our many ward families: Thank you for loving us even though we can't make Jell-O.

To our sista Mia Maids: Y'all ain't maids, but you put in work (the check is in the mail), and we appreciate it: Jen, Karin, Karyn, Kendra, Mama, Margaret, Maybelline, Nkoyo & Renee.

To our sistas that burned the midnight oil: Charly, Hailey, Kim, Syrétta.

To the mother of our sistahood, our Latter-day Saint Madea: Cathy. We hope you like us a whole lot more than you like flies! We love you.

SHOUT OUTS

To our DB posse: Laurel, who stalked us for a year and hid that we are cray cray. That's why we are kindred spirits. Chris, who spoke our language, no glossary needed. Liz, the ride-or-die backseat driver of our getaway car. Jerri, who made sure the black was always put back.

To our supersecret agent, Suzanne: James Bond ain't got nuttin' on you.

A special thanks to our Sistas in Zion followers, readers & listeners.

We've said it before, and we'll say it again: Gratitude and love to our husbands, children, and families for doing the laundry and all the other dirty work while we had our noses in this book.

Thank you, God, for continually reminding us that we are way too blessed to be stressed.

Photo by Sam Featherstone Photography

ABOUT THE SISTAS

TAMU SMITH and ZANDRA VRANES are popular multimedia personalities, the authors of the online blog SISTASinZION.com, and are the producers of the popular Latter-day Saint film *Jane and Emma*. Their media entities, which focus on humorous aspects of faith and religious culture, seek to uplift, inspire, bridge religious divides, and create healthy dialogue.